M000034056

Data Analysis and Probability Workbook

PEARSON

Prentice Hall

Boston, Massachusetts
Upper Saddle River, New Jersey

ISBN: 0-13-165725-9

4 5 6 7 8 9 10   09 08

Table of Contents

Name _____ Class _____ Date _____

Frequency Tables, Line Plots, and Histograms

Aimee asked students in her grade how many CDs they own. She displayed her data in a **frequency table**. Each tally stands for 1 CD.

Students' CD Collections

Number of CDs	17	18	19	20	21	22	23	24
Tally	⊮I	I	⊮	III	I	IIII	II	IIII
Frequency	6	1	5	3	1	4	2	4

She displayed the same data in a **line plot**. Each ✗ stands for 1 CD.

Number of CDs Students Own

```
✗
✗       ✗
✗       ✗           ✗       ✗
✗       ✗   ✗       ✗       ✗
✗       ✗   ✗       ✗   ✗   ✗
✗   ✗   ✗   ✗   ✗   ✗   ✗   ✗
───────────────────────────────
17  18  19  20  21  22  23  24
```

She also made a **histogram** to show the frequencies. The bars represent intervals of equal size. The height of each bar gives the frequency of the data.

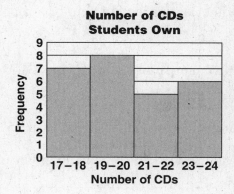

Number of CDs Students Own

Use the frequency table for Exercises 1–3.

1. Ms. Ortiz's class is planning a school garden. She asked her students how many rose bushes they want in the garden. She recorded the data in a frequency table. Complete the table.

2. Use the frequency table to make a line plot for the data.

3. Draw a histogram of the students' data.

Number of Rose Bushes	1	2	3	4	5	6
Tally	I	IIII	III	⊮I	I	I
Frequency						

Practice: Frequency Tables, Line Plots, and Histograms

Make a line plot for the data.

1. boxes of juice sold per day:

26 21 26 24 27 23 24 22

26 21 23 26 24 26 23

Ms. Makita made a line plot to show the scores her students got on a test. At the right is Ms. Makita's line plot.

2. What does each data item or ✗ represent?

_____

3. How many more students scored 75 than scored 95?

_____

4. How many students scored over 85? _____

5. What scores did the same number of students get?

_____

Test Scores

```
✗            ✗
✗   ✗   ✗   ✗
✗   ✗   ✗   ✗           ✗
✗   ✗   ✗   ✗   ✗   ✗
✗   ✗   ✗   ✗   ✗   ✗
✗   ✗   ✗   ✗   ✗   ✗
```
75 80 85 90 95 100

Nathan asked 24 classmates to estimate the total number of hours (to the nearest quarter hour) they spend doing homework Monday through Thursday. The frequency table below shows their responses.

6. Can you tell from the table how many students do homework for two hours or less? Explain. _____

_____

7. How many more students do homework for at least 5 h than do homework for less than 4 h? _____

8. Make a histogram for the data. Use the intervals in the table.

Hours Spent Doing Homework

Number of Hours	Frequency
1 – 1.75	1
2 – 2.75	1
3 – 3.75	2
4 – 4.75	6
5 – 5.75	8
6 – 6.75	3
7 – 7.75	2
8 – 8.75	1

Name _____ Class _____ Date _____

Reteaching 1: Frequency Tables and Line Plots

Use the data in the rainfall table to make a frequency table and a line plot for Albuquerque.

Inches	0	1	2
Frequency	2	9	1

The numbers of inches are 0, 1, 2, so these are listed in the top row. Since two months have 0 inches (less than 0.5 in.), the frequency is 2. Albuquerque has one inch of rainfall in 9 different months, so the frequency is 9. Similarly, the frequency for 2 inches is 1.

To draw a line plot, start with a number line. Label 0, 1, and 2 inches. Then make the appropriate number of ✗'s above each number. Be sure to line up your ✗'s across from each other.

Average Monthly Rainfall (in.)

City	Month											
	J	F	M	A	M	J	J	A	S	O	N	D
Albuquerque, NM	0	1	1	1	1	1	1	2	1	1	0	1
Charleston, SC	4	3	4	3	4	6	7	7	5	3	3	3
San Francisco, CA	4	3	3	1	0	0	0	0	0	1	3	3
Wilmington, DE	3	3	3	3	4	4	4	3	3	3	3	4

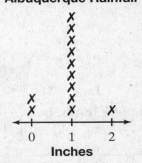

Albuquerque Rainfall

Use the data in the rainfall table to make a frequency table and a line plot for each city.

1. Charleston, SC

Inches					
Frequency					

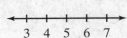

Charleston Rainfall

2. San Francisco, CA

Inches					
Frequency					

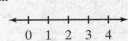

San Francisco Rainfall

3. Wilmington, DE

Inches		
Frequency		

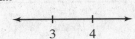

Wilmington Rainfall

Reteaching 2: Frequency Distributions

Data is often best organized in a table. A frequency distribution table shows the number of occurrences of a particular measurement.

1. Complete the frequency distribution.

Scores on History Test
84, 73, 99, 75, 82, 91, 87, 71, 83, 68, 94, 82, 88, 71, 75, 100, 80, 75, 67, 77, 90, 94, 81, 81, 70

Interval	Tally	Frequency
95–100		
90–94		
85–89		
80–84		
75–79		
70–74		
under 70		

2. Complete the frequency distribution. Use an interval of 50, start with 700–749, and end with "1000 and over."

Yards Gained Rushing
877, 915, 804, 889, 1366, 744, 1505, 702, 888, 991, 946, 750, 799, 891, 764, 900, 2001, 851, 777, 990, 700, 843, 922, 918

Interval	Tally	Frequency

3. Complete the frequency distribution. Use an interval of 20, start with 60–79, and end with "180 and over."

Annual Rainfall
99, 103, 141, 84, 77, 149, 124, 116, 80, 211, 66, 119, 189, 84, 107, 116, 155, 175, 61, 68, 82, 91, 120, 158, 102, 87

Interval	Tally	Frequency

Reteaching 3: Histograms

The **frequency** of a data item is the number of times it appears. A **frequency table** provides intervals, then tallies each data item in its interval.

Telephone Numbers (Last Four Digits)

9782	8609	7880	9012	5620	1190	2324	2568
9877	4085	6856	7367	3642	6784	8015	7761
9001	4227	7452	9811	4326	6433	4228	8111

The last four digits of 24 phone numbers were chosen from a phone book.

Make a frequency table for the data.

① Choose an appropriate interval. All intervals must be the same size.

② Mark tallies and write totals for the data.

Telephone Numbers

Last Four Digits	Tally	Frequency
1000–1999	I	1
2000–2999	II	2
3000–3999	I	1
4000–4999	IIII	4
5000–5999	I	1
6000–6999	III	3
7000–7999	IIII	4
8000–8999	III	3
9000–9999	IIIII	5

You can use a frequency table to make a **histogram.**

In a histogram, there is no space between the bars.

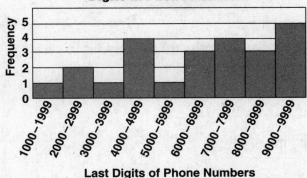

Digits in Phone Numbers

Last Digits of Phone Numbers

Use the following data for Exercises 1 and 2.

Raisins in a small box: 33 32 30 40 29 35
36 33 42 28 41 39 30 29 35 40 33 34 31 28

1. Make a frequency table for the data.

2. Use your frequency table to make a histogram.

Making Bar and Line Graphs

To make bar graphs and line graphs from data, follow these steps:

① Give the graph a title. Decide what information to show on each axis.

Number of Apples Picked

Week	Apples
1	21
2	34
3	29

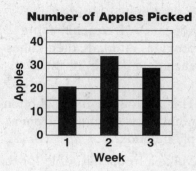

② Draw and label the horizontal and vertical axes.

③ Choose a scale. Think about which intervals of 5, 10, 100, or 1,000 would work best.

Amount Earned from After-School Job

Week	Amount
1	$10.00
2	$9.00
3	$12.00
4	$15.00

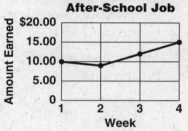

④ Draw each bar, or plot the data and connect the points to form a line graph.

Would the best scale for the given data be fives, tens, hundreds, or thousands?

1. 83 ft, 49 ft, 66 ft, 73 ft

   _____

2. $12, $22, $18, $26, $6

   _____

3. 1,000 mi; 2,500 mi; 4,000 mi

   _____

4. 320 lb, 179 lb, 240 lb, 119 lb

   _____

5. 6 days, 10 days, 4 days, 9 days

   _____

6. 66 gal, 34 gal, 71 gal, 59 gal

   _____

Use the tables at the right for Exercises 7 and 8.

7. Would you use a bar graph or line graph to display the data in the table? Explain your choice.

   _____

   _____

Favorite Sports

Sport	Number Answering
Wrestling	290
Football	50
Basketball	520
Baseball	130

8. Would you use a bar graph or line graph for the data? Explain.

   _____

   _____

Population of Springdale

Year	Population
1980	45,000
1990	62,000
2000	68,000

Practice: Bar and Line Graphs

Use the table below to answer Exercises 1–3.

All-Time Favorite Sports Figures

Sports Figure	Number of Votes
Babe Ruth	29
Babe Didrikson Zaharias	22
Jackie Robinson	18
Billie Jean Moffitt King	17
Muhammad Ali	14
Jim Thorpe	13

Source: *The Book of Lists #3, The People's Almanac*

1. What would you label the horizontal axis for a bar graph of the data?

_____

2. What interval would you use for the vertical axis of the bar graph?

_____

3. Construct a bar graph displaying the number of votes for all-time favorite sports figures.

Use the table below to answer Exercises 4 and 5.

Daily Use of Petroleum in the U.S.
   (millions of barrels)

Year	Number
1960	1.7
1965	1.9
1970	2.2
1975	1.9
1980	1.5
1985	1.3
1990	1.1
1995	1.1
2000	1.2

SOURCE: U.S. Dept. of Energy,
Annual Energy Review

4. Construct a line graph for the amount of petroleum used daily in the U.S.

5. What overall trend does the line graph show?

_____

_____

Stacked Bar and Multiple Line Graphs

A **stacked bar graph** has bars that are divided into categories. Each bar represents the total of the categories.

Sports Team Members		
Grade	**Boys**	**Girls**
6	57	44
7	78	50
8	39	48

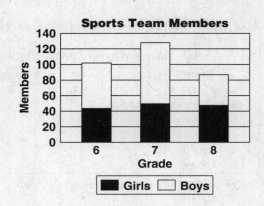

A **multiple line graph** shows more than one category changing over time.

Cafeteria Sales, 1992–1995 (in Thousands of Items)		
Year	**Burgers**	**Salads**
1992	11	4
1993	9	7
1994	6	10
1995	4	12

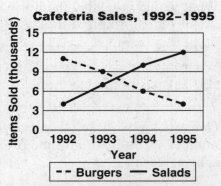

Use the stacked bar graph above for Exercises 1–3.

1. In which grade is there the greatest total participation?

   _____

2. Which grade has the greatest difference between the number of boys and girls participating? the least difference?

   _____

3. Explain how you can find the number for the top category of a bar in a stacked bar graph.

Use the multiple line graph above for Exercises 4–5.

4. In which year were the numbers of burgers and salads that were sold closest to one another?

   _____

5. How can you find the total number of burgers and salads sold in any one year?

   _____

Name _____ Class _____ Date _____

Practice: Multiple Bar and Line Graphs

•••

Use this TV viewing data for Exercises 1–4.

Average Viewing Time 8:00 P.M.–11:00 P.M. (Mon.–Sun.)		
Age Group	Male	Female
18–24	6 h 40 min	7 h 42 min
25–54	9 h 23 min	10 h 3 min
55+	12 h 19 min	13 h 7 min

Source: *Nielson Media Research*

1. Make a sliding bar graph where each bar represents an age group.

2. Make a double bar graph.

3. In which graph is it easier to compare the viewing times within each age group? _____

4. In which graph is it easier to compare the viewing times within each gender? _____

Use data from this table for Exercises 5–7.

Population (100,000s)

Year	Hialeah, FL	Birmingham, AL
1960	1.7	3.4
1970	1.0	3.0
1980	1.5	2.8
1990	1.9	2.7
2000	2.3	2.4

SOURCE: U.S. Bureau of the Census

5. Make a stacked bar graph. Let each bar represent a year.

6. Make a multiple line graph.

7. In which graph is it easier to see which city's population has changed the most? _____

Name _____ Class _____ Date _____

Circle Graphs

The class took a survey of favorite foods.
The results are shown in the table and the circle graph.

To make a circle graph:

① Find the total number of votes.

② Find each part of the total as a fraction or percent.

③ Find the measure of each central angle in the circle graph.

④ Draw, label, and title the graph.

Food	Votes	② Fraction	%	③ Degrees
Burgers	8	$\frac{8}{48} = \frac{1}{6}$	$16\frac{2}{3}$%	60°
Pizza	16	$\frac{1}{3}$	$33\frac{1}{3}$%	120°
Steak	6	$\frac{1}{8}$	$12\frac{1}{2}$%	45°
Tacos	12	$\frac{1}{4}$	25%	90°
Pasta	6	$\frac{1}{8}$	$12\frac{1}{2}$%	45°
Total	① 48			360°

Favorite Foods

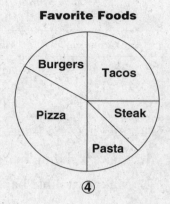

④

**Find the measure of the central angle that represents
each fraction or percent in a circle graph.**

1. $\frac{1}{5}$ _____

2. 40% _____

3. $\frac{1}{2}$ _____

4. 5% _____

5. 35% _____

6. $\frac{1}{10}$ _____

7. 20% _____

8. $\frac{1}{12}$ _____

Display the data in each table in a circle graph.

9. a monthly family budget

10. number of children per family

Monthly Family Budget	
Item	**Amount**
Rent	$425
Food	$150
Clothes	$50
Gas	$75
Phone	$25
Misc.	$100

Children per Family	
Children	**Families**
0	4
1	15
2	20
3	13
4	5
5	3

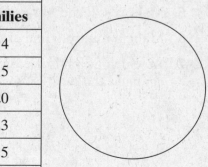

Name _____ Class _____ Date _____

Practice: Circle Graphs

• •

**The Rahman family has a budget for their summer vacation.
Complete the table below. Use the results to construct a
circle graph.**

	Category	Amount Budgeted	Percent of Total	Degrees in Central Angle
1.	Gas	$200		
2.	Meals	$400		
3.	Motels	$600		
4.	Other	$800		

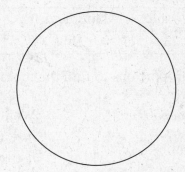

**Lucy has set up a budget. Complete the table below. Use the
results to construct a circle graph.**

	Category	Amount Budgeted	Percent of Total	Degrees in Central Angle
5.	Clothing	$50		
6.	Entertainment	$40		
7.	Savings	$25		
8.	Transportation	$10		

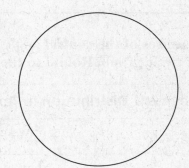

9. A dairy association surveyed customers to
find out whether they were drinking more
milk than they were a year ago. Here is how
they responded. Display the responses in a
circle graph.

more	56.3%
the same	20.5%
less	10.1%
not sure	13.1%

• •

Reteaching: Circle Graphs

Find the measures of the central angles that you would draw to represent each percent in a circle graph. Round to the nearest degree.

Employment Distribution in California				
Service	Trade	Manufacturing	Government	Other
31%	23%	15%	17%	14%

You can use proportions to find the measures of the central angles. You also can use equations.

What is 31% of 360?

$n = (0.31)(360)$

$n = 112°$

What is 23% of 360?

$n = (0.23)(360)$

$n = 83°$

What is 15% of 360?

$n = (0.15)(360)$

$n = 54°$

What is 17% of 360?

$n = (0.17)(360)$

$n = 61°$

What is 14% of 360?

$n = (0.14)(360)$

$n = 50°$

Find the measures of the central angle that you would draw to represent each percent in a circle graph. Round to the nearest degree.

Measure of central angle

	Employment Distribution in Texas	
1.	Service	27%
2.	Trade	24%
3.	Manufacturing	13%
4.	Government	18%
5.	Other	18%

1. _____

2. _____

3. _____

4. _____

5. _____

Stem-and-Leaf Plots

• •

A **stem-and-leaf** plot is an easy way to show data arranged
in order.

**8th Grade 100-M Dash
(Times to Nearest 0.1 s)**

13.1	16.2	15.5	15.2	13.5
15.3	14.8	14.4	17.5	12.2
14.1	16.1	16.9	15.3	16.8
16.0	15.3	12.0	18.2	14.6
13.2	18.3	16.6	15.3	18.8

① Choose *stems*. The times range from
12.0 to 18.8. Choose 12 to 18 as stems.

② List the tenths digits as *leaves*.

18	2 3 8
17	5
16	0 1 2 6 8 9
15	2 3 3 3 3 5
14	1 4 6 8
13	1 2 5
12	0 2

③ Make a key to explain what each stem
and leaf represents.

18 | 2 means 18.2

The **mode** is the most frequent number.
The mode is 15.3 seconds.

The **range** is the greatest number minus the least number.
The range is 18.8 − 12.0 = 6.8 seconds.

The **median** is the middle number or average of the middle two
numbers. The median is 15.3 seconds.

---

1. Complete the stem-and-leaf plot for the data.

**8th Grade 200-M Dash
(Times to Nearest 0.1 s)**

32.5	32.1	38.5	31.7	34.7
29.3	35.2	34.4	30.2	35.3
34.7	31.9	36.0	32.2	36.7
32.2	31.4	34.7	29.5	36.9
36.4	33.4	38.6	34.7	37.3

Times for the 200-M Dash

38	_____
37	_____
36	_____
35	_____
34	_____
33	_____
32	_____
31	_____
30	_____
29	_____

Use your stem-and-leaf plot for Exercises 2–5.

2. The mode is _____.   **3.** The range is _____.   **4.** The median is _____.

5. How many 8th grade students finished the race in less than 35 s?

_____

• •

Practice: Stem-and-Leaf Plots

The stem-and-leaf plot at the right shows
the bowling scores for 20 bowlers.
Use the plot for Exercises 1–3.

10	0 2 2 4 4 4
11	1 3 5 5 5 9
12	4 5 9 9
13	0 6 8 8

13 | 8 means 138

1. What numbers make up the stems?

_____

2. What are the leaves for the stem 12?

_____

3. Find the median, mode, and range.

_____

Make a stem-and-leaf plot for each set of data. Then find
the median, mode, and range.

4. 8 19 27 36 35 24 6 15 16 24 38 23 20

_____

5. 8.6 9.1 7.4 6.3 8.2 9.0 7.5 7.9 6.3 8.1 7.1 8.2 7.0 9.6 9.9

_____

6. 436 521 470 586 692 634 417 675 526 719 817

_____

7. 17.9 20.4 18.6 19.5 17.6 18.5 17.4 18.5 19.4

_____

The back-to-back stem-and-leaf plot at
the right shows the high and low
temperatures for a week in a certain
city. Use this plot for Exercises 8–10.

Temperature

Low		High
8 7	5	
4 3	6	5 9 9
2 1 0	7	2 5 6
	8	0

63 ← 3 | 6 | 2 → 62

8. Find the range for the high temperatures.

_____

9. Find the median for the low temperatures.

_____

10. Find the mode for the high temperatures.

_____

11. Make a back-to-back stem-and-leaf plot for the following data.
Find the median and mode for each set of data.

Set A: 75 82 79 80 75 76 83 74 75 86 80 71 75 _____

Set B: 71 73 75 80 79 80 74 80 74 79 76 80 81 _____

Reteaching: Stem-and-Leaf Plots

Make a **stem-and-leaf plot** of the summer earnings data.

① Make a column of the tens digits of the data in order from least to greatest. These are the stems.

② Record the ones digits for each tens digit in order from least to greatest. These are the leaves.

③ Make a *key* to explain what the stems and leaves represent.

The **range** of a set of data is the difference between the greatest value (58) and the least value (12).

The range of the summer earnings is $58 - 12 = 46$, or $46.

Daily Summer Earnings					
$35	$35	$38	$15	$52	$40
$20	$23	$56	$12	$14	$58

```
① stems        ② leaves
    1            1 | 2 4 5
    2            2 | 0 3
    3            3 | 5 5 8
    4            4 | 0
    5            5 | 2 6 8

            1 | 2 means 12
```

---

1. Complete the stem-and-leaf plot of this set of data.

24	36	64	42	59
61	16	63	54	39
36	45	15	27	51

```
1 |
2 | 4
3 | 6
4 |
5 |
6 |
```

2. Use the stem-and-leaf plot you made to find the greatest value, least value, and range of the data.

_____

3. Brandy recorded these high temperatures for two weeks in July. Make a stem-and-leaf plot of her data. Find the range.

92	86	91	90	85
82	84	78	79	83
84	89	86	87	

4. Mr. Wang recorded these test scores. Make a stem-and-leaf plot of the data. Find the range.

66	83	58	65	66
66	82	55	57	71
40	43	41	56	71
74	81	85	63	62

The range is _____ .

The range is _____ .

Activity: Relating Stem-and-Leaf Plots to Histograms

A stem-and-leaf plot organizes data. A frequency table presents the same data in a more condensed form. A histogram shows the same data on a bar graph.

In the spaces below, complete the stem-and-leaf plot, the frequency table, and the histogram to show the following data.

Team	A	B	C	D	E	F	G	H	I	J	K	L	M	N
Score	46	68	32	44	79	37	63	44	58	57	61	47	76	64

a.
Stem	Leaf
3	_____
4	_____
5	_____
6	_____
7	_____

b.

Frequency Table

Grouping Intervals	Frequency
30–39	_____
40–49	_____
50–59	_____
_____	_____
_____	_____

c.

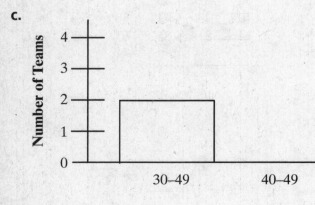

Puzzle: Keeping Score

At a recent gymnastics meet, someone spilled water
on the left side of the official score card. All
whole numbers were erased, but the decimal portions
of all scores were legible. Part of the scorecard
is at the right. Use the clues to reconstruct the
scores. Read all clues before you begin. Record your
answers on the stem-and-leaf plot below.

1. Judge A recalls that the decimal portions of 4 of
   the 5 scores that began with 7 were multiples
   of 10.

2. Judge B recalls that the decimal portion of all 3 of
   the scores that began with 6 were multiples of
   15 or 7.

3. Judge C recalls that there was a .75 in each stem
   on the stem-and-leaf table below.

4. Judge D recalls that the 3 scores that began with
   8 were identical.

5. Judge E recalls that the decimal portion of both
   scores that began with 5 were equal to or greater
   than .75.

	.75
	.35
	.45
	.50
	.75
	.75
	.75
	.20
	.90
	.75
	.75
	.50
	.40

Stem	Leaf
5	
6	
7	
8	

Box-and-Whisker Plots

Make a box-and-whisker plot for the data set.

Percent of Federally Owned Land in Ten Western States				
45%	24%	52%	61%	28%
42%	34%	48%	63%	36%

Step 1: First list the data in order from least to greatest. Find the median.

24 28 34 36 42 | 45 48 52 61 63

Since there is an even number of percents (10), there are two middle numbers. Add them and divide by 2.

$\frac{42 + 45}{2} = \frac{87}{2} = 43.5$ The median is 43.5.

Step 2: Find the upper and lower quartiles.

The lower quartile is the median of the lower half.   24 28 $\boxed{34}$ 36 42
The lower quartile is 34.

The upper quartile is the median of the upper half.   45 48 $\boxed{52}$ 61 63
The upper quartile is 52.

Step 3: Draw a number line. Mark the least and greatest values, the median, and the quartiles. Draw a box from the first to the third quartiles. Draw whiskers from the least and greatest values to the box.

The data range from 24 to 63. A scale of 5 from 20 to 70 would have 11 marks.

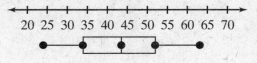

Make a box-and-whisker plot for each data set.

1. area in 1,000 mi² of 13 western states

122	164	71	98	84	147	114
111	98	85	104	71	77	

median: _____

lower quartile: _____

upper quartile: _____

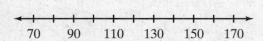

2. percent of area that is inland water for 11 northeastern states

13%	4%	26%	4%	32%	13%
15%	3%	21%	7%	21%	

median: _____

lower quartile: _____

upper quartile: _____

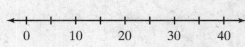

Name _____ Class _____ Date _____

Practice: Box-and-Whisker Plots

Use the box-and-whisker plot to answer each question.

Weekly Mileage Totals, 24 Runners

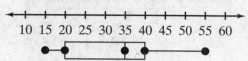

1. What is the highest weekly total? _____ the lowest? _____

2. What is the median weekly total? _____

3. What percent of runners run less than 40 miles a week? _____

4. How many runners run less than 20 miles a week? _____

Make a box-and-whisker plot for each set of data.

5. 16 20 30 15 23 11 15 21 30 29 13 16

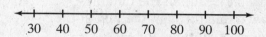

6. 9 12 10 3 2 3 9 11 5 1 10 4 7 12 3 10

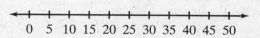

7. 70 77 67 65 79 82 70 68 75 73 69 66
70 73 89 72

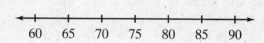

Use box-and-whisker plots to compare data sets. Use a single number line for each comparison.

8. 1st set: 7 12 25 3 1 29 30 7 15 2 5
10 29 1 10 30 18 8 7 29
2nd set: 37 17 14 43 27 19 32 1 8 48
26 16 28 6 25 18

1st Set

2nd Set

9. area in 1,000 mi^2
midwestern states:
45 36 58 97 56 65 87 82 77
southern states:
52 59 48 52 42 32 54 43 70 53 66

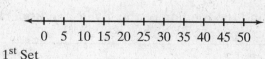

Midwestern
States

Southern
States

Reteaching: Box-and-Whisker Plots

A **box-and-whisker plot** shows the distribution of data along a number line. Make a box-and-whisker plot for the data in the table at the right.

Letters per Word in a Newspaper Article (30-Word Sample)					
9	4	2	11	1	8
8	2	6	1	7	3
3	3	8	6	8	5
2	7	8	9	2	4
7	1	6	14	8	4

① Order the data:
   1 1 1 2 2 2 2 3 3 3 4 4 4 5 6 6 6 7 7 7 8 8 8 8 8 8 9 9 1 1 1 4

② Find the median. The median is 6.

③ Find the medians of the lower and upper halves of the data.
   (lower) 1 1 1 2 2 2 2 **3** 3 3 4 4 4 5 6
   (upper) 6 6 7 7 7 8 8 **8** 8 8 8 9 9 11 14

④ Mark the least and greatest values below a number line. Mark the three medians.

⑤ Draw a box connecting the lower and upper medians. This box shows where at least half the data lies. Draw a line through the box at the median of all the data.

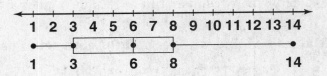

⑥ Draw whiskers from the box to the least and greatest values.

Complete the steps to make a box-and-whisker plot for the data.

1. Order the data.

   _____

2. Find the median.

   _____

3. Find the median of the lower and upper halves.

   _____

4. Draw the box-and-whisker plot.

   1 2 3 4 5 6 7 8 9 10 11 12 13

Letters per Word in a Magazine Article (30-Word Sample)				
3	7	8	3	7
4	6	4	3	7
3	1	13	3	2
8	8	2	11	5
5	3	9	9	2
3	2	10	3	2

Reading and Understanding Graphs

A **bar graph** helps to compare data. To read the graph at the right, first read the horizontal axis. Then read from the top of a bar to the vertical axis. This graph shows that in September, Miss Foster's class read 25 books.

Books Read by Miss Foster's Class

A **circle graph** shows how parts compare to a whole. The graph at the right shows that 27 people in the survey speak English at home.

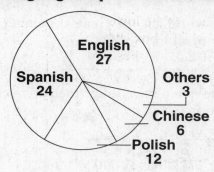

Languages Spoken at Home

Use the bar graph for Exercises 1–4.

1. How many books were read in December?

_____

2. In which month did students read the most books?

_____

3. How many more books were read in January than in October?

_____

4. In which 2 months did students read the same number of books?

_____

Use the circle graph for Exercises 5–8.

5. Which 2 languages did most people surveyed speak?

_____

6. How many people spoke Polish?

_____

7. How many more people spoke Spanish than Polish?

_____

8. Did more people speak Polish or Chinese?

_____

Name _____ Class _____ Date _____

Practice: Reading and Understanding Graphs

Use the circle graph for Exercises 1–3.

1. Which element is found in the greatest quantity in the body?

_____

2. What are the three elements named?

_____

3. Why might there be a portion labeled "other"?

_____

_____

Major Elements Found in the Body

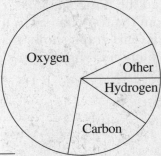

Use the bar graph for Exercises 4–6.

4. Which part of the world has the greatest number of operating nuclear reactors?

_____

5. Which parts of the world have fewer than 40 nuclear reactors in operation?

_____

6. Which part of the world has about 20% more nuclear reactors in operation as the Far East?

_____

Nuclear Reactors in Operation

Number of Reactors

175
150
125
100
75
50
25

N. America S. & Central Am. W. Europe E. Europe Mid. East Africa Far East

Region

Use the line graph for Exercises 7 and 8.

7. What overall trend does the line graph show?

_____

_____

_____

8. During which 10-year period did the percent of unmarried men, ages 25–29, decrease?

_____

Men Aged 25–29 Who Have Never Married

Men Never Married (%)

60

40

20

1960 1970 1980 1990 2000

Year

Choose A, B, C, or D. Which type of graph—circle, bar, or line—would be most appropriate to display the data?

9. the height of a child from ages 1 to 6
   A. circle graph   **B.** bar graph   **C.** line graph   **D.** any graph

Reading Graphs Critically

Two important factors in determining whether a graph gives a correct impression of data are:

- How the scale is chosen;
- Whether the entire scale is shown.

The data at the right can be shown in a bar graph.

Countries With Most Universities

India	8407
United States	5758

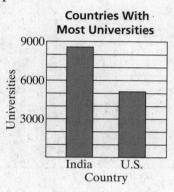

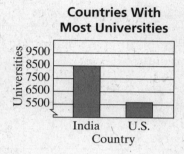

In the first graph, the scale is in multiples of 1,000. The entire scale from 0 through 8,000 is shown. The graph accurately compares the numbers of universities in the two countries.

In the second graph, the scale is in multiples of 500. There is a break in the vertical scale. The graph can imply a misleading comparison between the two countries.

Use the bar graphs above to answer the questions.

1. From which graph is it easier to tell that India has about twice the number of universities as the United States?

   _____

2. In the second graph, about how many times the number of U.S. universities does India *appear* to have?

   _____

3. Which graph makes it easier to estimate the number of universities in each country? Why?

   _____

   _____

   _____

4. Why does the second graph give a misleading impression of the data?

   _____

   _____

   _____

Name _____ Class _____ Date _____

Practice: Reading Graphs Critically

Use the graph at the right for Exercises 1–4.

1. Which age group appears to have about fourteen times as many people as the number of people in the 15–24 age group?

   _____

2. Which age group actually has about seven times as many people living alone as the 15–24 age group?

   _____

3. Draw a new bar graph to give an accurate impression of the data.

4. Explain why you chose to draw the graph as you have.

   _____

   _____

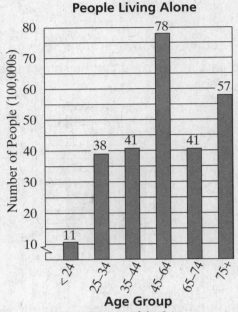

People Living Alone

SOURCE: U.S. Bureau of the Census

5. Use the data below to draw a graph that exaggerates the popularity of all-time favorite TV shows.

Show	Households Watching (100,000s)
M*A*S*H	50
Dallas	41
Roots Part VIII	36
Super Bowl XVI	40

SOURCE: A.C. Nielson estimates.

6. Draw a graph that gives an accurate impression of the data.

7. Explain why you chose to draw the graph as you have.

   _____

8. Give a reason someone might draw a graph of the information that is misleading. _____

   _____

Name _____ Class _____ Date _____

Activity: Organizing and Analyzing Data

Population Density

The table below lists the number of people per square mile in each of the 50 states and Washington, DC, as of 2000. These figures are known as population densities.

In order to organize these data into a usable form, consider these questions.

Population Densities (per square mile)							
State	**Density**	**State**	**Density**	**State**	**Density**	**State**	**Density**
Ala.	88	Ill.	225	Mon.	6	R.I.	1013
Alaska	1	Ind.	171	Neb.	22	S.C.	135
Ariz.	47	Iowa	52	Nev.	19	S.D.	10
Ark.	52	Kans.	33	N.H.	140	Tenn.	139
Calif.	221	Ky.	102	N.J.	1144	Tex.	82
Colo.	43	La.	103	N. Mex.	15	Utah	28
Conn.	707	Maine	42	N.Y.	403	Vt.	66
Del.	408	Md.	550	N.C.	168	Va.	182
D.C.	9313	Mass.	814	N. Dak.	9	Wash.	90
Fla.	304	Mich.	176	Ohio	278	W. Va.	75
Ga.	145	Minn.	63	Okla.	50	Wis.	100
Hawaii	191	Miss.	61	Oreg.	36	Wyo.	5
Ida.	16	Mo.	82	Pa.	274		

1. Does it appear that the data can easily be organized into a stem-and-leaf plot? Why or why not?

_____

2. If your answer to question 1 was no, which densities would prevent a stem-and-leaf plot from being useful?

_____

3. What would be an appropriate frequency interval if you were going to complete a frequency table for all the data?

_____

4. What incorrect impression might you give about Washington, D.C., and New Jersey if your highest interval were "1,000 or more"?

_____

5. What could you do on the frequency table or in a histogram to avoid creating that wrong impression?

_____

6. What would you be able to tell about the total population of each state after making a frequency table and histogram from these data?

_____

Scatter Plots and Trends

Gilbert is investigating the relationship between the number of credit cards a person has and the amount of credit card debt.

First, he made a table of his data.

Then he plotted the data in a scatter plot.

Credit Cards and Credit Card Debt

Number of Cards	Amount of Debt
1	$0
1	$1,000
1	$5,000
2	$3,000
2	$5,000
3	$10,000
3	$5,000
3	$8,000
4	$10,000
5	$19,000

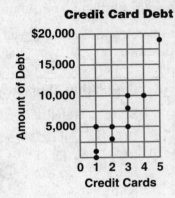

Gilbert's scatter plot shows a **positive trend** in the data. That means as the number of credit cards goes up so does the amount of debt. As one value goes up, so does the other.

In a **negative trend,** one value goes up while the other goes down.

---

1. Dana surveyed her friends about how much TV they watch and their average test scores. Her results are shown below. Complete the scatter plot for the data.

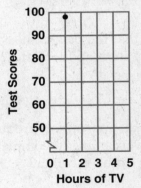

Test Scores and TV

TV Hours Per Day	Average Test Score	TV Hours Per Day	Average Test Score
1	98	3	79
1	86	3	73
2	90	3	75
2	82	4	62
2	85	5	68

2. Is the trend in the data negative or positive? Explain.

_____

3. Describe the relationship Dana likely found between test scores and TV time.

_____

Practice: Making Predictions from Scatter Plots
••

Tell whether a scatter plot made for each set of data would show a positive trend, a negative trend, or no trend.

1. amount of education and annual salary

_____

2. weight and speed in a foot race

_____

3. test score and shoe size

_____

For the scatter plots in Exercises 4 and 5, use a computer or graph the points by hand.

4. Make a scatter plot showing the number of homeowners on one axis and vacation homeowners on the other axis. If there is a trend, draw a trend line.

Residents of Maintown

Year	Homeowners	Vacation Homeowners
1997–98	2,050	973
1996–97	1,987	967
1995–96	1,948	1,041
1994–95	1,897	1,043
1993–94	1,862	1,125
1992–93	1,832	1,126

5. Draw the data in a scatter plot. If there is a trend, draw a trend line.

Time Spent Studying (minutes)	Number of Words Spelled Correctly
40	20
35	18
32	16
30	16
20	15
15	15
10	10
10	8

6. Wynetta found the graph shown at the right. The title of the graph was missing. What could the graph be describing?

_____

_____

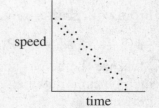

Activity 1: Making a Scatter Plot

Materials: Ruler, tape measure

In this activity, you will make a scatter plot to show the relationship between two variable quantities.

To understand the procedure read the table below, listing the number of minutes several students spent studying for a math test and the scores they achieved on the test. Then look at the *scatter plot* based on this table.

Students	1	2	3	4	5	6	7	8	9
Study time (in min.)	20	65	30	90	45	30	80	50	35
Test score	60	85	70	100	88	77	90	82	80

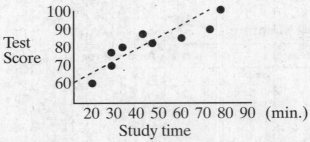

The straight dotted line in the scatter plot shows the *line of best fit* of the given data. It is the line that the data points cluster about. Since the slope of this line is positive, there is a *positive* correlation between study times and test scores. A negative slope indicates a *negative* correlation between the times and scores. If the data do not cluster about any single line, they are *unrelated*.

Split into groups of between 7 and 9 students. Each group will make a scatter plot of foot length and height (in either centimeters or inches) of the students in the group.

1. With a ruler, measure the length of the right foot of each group member, and with a tape measure, determine the height of each student. Fill in the data you find in the following table.

Students	1	2	3	4	5	6	7	8	9
Foot length									
Height									

2. Make a scatter plot of the data: Mark foot lengths on the vertical axis and heights on the horizontal axis. Plot the values you wrote down in the table above.

3. From your scatter plot, is there a correlation between foot length and height?

   _____ If so, is it positive? _____

4. Measure the height and the circumference of the head of each group member and make a scatter plot of these data. Is there a positive correlation between the data? _____

Activity 2: Making a Scatter Plot

In this activity, you will make scatter plots using some climatological data from U.S. cities. The table below gives the average temperature and average precipitation in the month of March for various U.S. cities, together with the latitude of those cities.

City	Av. March Temp (°F)	Av. March Precip. (in.)	Latitude (°N)
Atlanta, GA	53	5.9	34
Boston, MA	38	4.1	42
Buffalo, NY	33	3.0	43
Dallas, TX	56	2.4	33
Houston, TX	61	2.7	30
Kansas City, MO	42	2.1	39
Lexington, KY	44	4.8	38
Los Angeles, CA	60	2.4	34
Miami, FL	72	1.9	26
Nashville, TN	49	5.6	36

1. Make a scatter plot of temperature against latitude, using the data from the table.

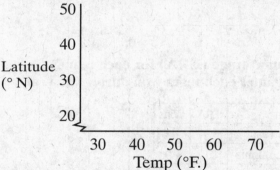

2. Is there a correlation between temperature and latitude? _____
   If so, is it positive? _____

3. On the axes below, make a scatter plot of precipitation against latitude, using the data above.

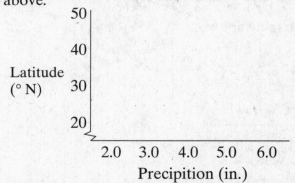

4. Is there a correlation between precipitation and latitude? _____
   If so, is it positive? _____

Name _____ Class _____ Date _____

Analyzing Scatter Plots
• •

Tell whether the variables in each scatter plot are positively correlated, negatively correlated, or unrelated.

1. _____

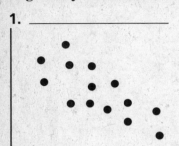

2. _____

3. _____

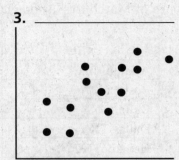

Tell whether each pair of quantities is positively correlated, negatively correlated, or not related.

4. traffic volume and commuting time _____

5. average outside temperature and amount of fuel used to heat a house
_____

6. hat size and average of math test scores _____

The table below lists combined earned run average (ERA) for each team's pitching staff in 2002 and the number of games each team won during the year.

Team	ERA	Wins	Team	ERA	Wins
Anaheim	3.69	99	Montreal	3.97	83
Arizona	3.92	98	Philadelphia	4.17	80
Boston	3.75	93	St. Louis	3.70	97
Chicago	4.55	81	Seattle	4.07	93
Cleveland	4.91	74	Tampa Bay	5.21	62
Houston	4.00	84	Texas	5.15	72

7a. Make a scatter plot of the data in the table above.

ERA
5.00
4.00
3.00

60 70 80 90 100
Wins

b. Are the variables in your scatter plot positively correlated, negatively correlated, or unrelated? _____

Reteaching: Scatter Plots and Trends

To make a scatter plot and find a trend for the data below:

① Choose a scale along each axis to represent the two sets of data.

② Locate the ordered pairs on the graph for the data.

③ Is there a trend? Do both sets of values increase? Does one decrease as the other increases? If neither occurs, there is no trend.

④ If there is a trend, draw a trend line that closely fits the data.

Age and Height Survey

Age (y)	Height (in.)	Age (y)	Height (in.)	Age (y)	Height (in.)
11	55	4	39	12	55
10	55	13	62	10	54
8	49	11	52	7	47
6	45	5	41	13	63
10	52	14	62	9	60
11	59	12	56	9	52
7	45	8	52	12	58
12	60	6	44	13	60
6	48	7	48	8	50
5	45	4	39	11	56

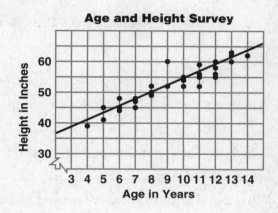

Use the data below to complete Exercises 1–5.

Weight (lb)	78	63	67	52	81	92	60	34	83	47	73	98	45	31	95	71	76	41
Height (in.)	56	52	55	47	58	60	50	39	58	45	54	61	45	36	60	54	56	41

1. Draw the scatter plot and a trend line.

2. Use your graph to estimate the height of a person who weighs about 90 lb.

   _____

3. Use your graph to estimate the weight of a student 51 in. tall.

   _____

4. Is there a relationship between height and weight? _____

5. Write a sentence to explain your answer to Exercise 4.

   _____

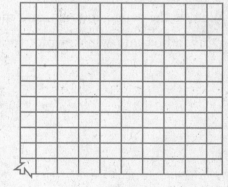

Assessment 1: Graphs

The histogram below shows the favorite summertime activity of each eighth-grade student at a certain school.

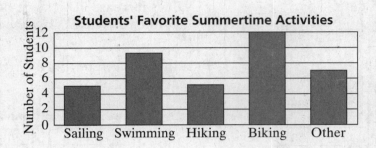

1. How many students' responses are shown in the graph? _____

2. Which activity is most popular? How many students chose that activity?
   _____

3. Which two activities are equally popular? How many students chose each of those activities? _____

4. What percent of the students chose swimming as their favorite summer activity? _____

5. Why is there an "Other" category? _____
   _____
   _____

A data set consists of the values {0, 10, 20, ... } and has a mean of 50.

6. What is the range, median, and mode? _____

7. Draw a box-and-whisker plot for the data.

Measures of Central Tendency

The **median** of this set of data is the middle value when the scores are ordered.

23 25 25 26 26 **26 26** 26 27 27 28 29

Since there are two middle scores, add them and divide by 2.

$$\frac{26 + 26}{2} = 26$$

The **mean** is the sum of the scores divided by the number of scores.

25 + 26 + 28 + 25 + 26 + 27 + 27 + 26 + 26 + 29 + 26 + 23 = 314

$\frac{314}{12} = 26.166667$, or about 26.2 pages

The **mode** is the score that occurs the most. The mode is 26 pages.

Number of Pages Read by Members of the Science Fiction Book Club			
25	26	28	25
26	27	27	26
26	29	26	23

Choose a calculator, pencil and paper, or mental math. Find the mean, median, and mode of each set of data.

1. movies seen: 3 3 1 4 0 4 2 5 7 4 1 2

_____

2. miles hiked: 5 10 9 12 8 4 5 7 5 13 11

_____

3. runs scored: 0 0 8 4 15 9 1 1 6 7 10 2

_____

4. costs of a ride:
$3.25 $2.50 $4.00 $4.00 $3.50 $2.00 $4.00 $3.00 $2.50
$3.00 $4.00

_____

Name the measure of central tendency you would report to your parents. Give your reason.

5. test scores: 89 84 79 80 81 55

_____

_____

6. friends' allowances: $10 $15 $12 $15 $8

_____

_____

Practice 1: Measures of Central Tendency

Choose a calculator, pencil and paper, or mental math.
Find the mean, median, and mode of each of the following.

1. hours of piano practice
_____

Hours Mr. Capelli's students practice

2 1 2 0 1 2 2 1 2 2

2. days of snow per month
_____

Monthly snow days in Central City

8 10 5 1 0 0 0 0 0 1 3 12

3. number of students per class
_____

Class size in Westmont Middle School

32 26 30 35 25 24 35 30 29 25

4. ratings given by students to a new movie
_____

Student ratings of a movie

10 9 10 8 9 7 5 3 8 9 9 10 9 9 7

5. points scored in five basketball games
_____

Points scored by Westmont JV

72 67 83 92 54

6. bowling scores for one bowler
_____

Li's bowling scores

129 136 201 146 154

What is the best measure of central tendency for each type
of data—mean, median, or mode? Explain.

7. most popular movie in the past month
_____
_____

8. favorite hobby
_____
_____

9. class size in a school
_____
_____

10. ages of members in a club
_____
_____

Each person has taken four tests and has one more test to
take. Find the score that each person must make to change
the mean or median as shown.

11. Barry has scores of 93, 84, 86, and 75.
He wants to raise the mean to 86.
_____

12. Liz has scores of 87, 75, 82, and 93.
She wants to raise the median to 87.
_____

13. Jim has scores of 60, 73, 82, and 75.
He wants to raise the mean to 75.
_____

14. Andrea has scores of 84, 73, 92, and 88.
She wants the median to be 86.
_____

Practice 2: Mean, Median, Mode and Outliers

The sum of the heights of all the students in Mrs. Maloney's class is 1,472 in.

1. The mean height is 5 ft 4 in. How many students are in the class? (1 ft = 12 in.) _____

2. The median height is 5 ft 2 in. How many students in Mrs. Maloney's class are 5 ft 2 in. or taller? _____

   How many are shorter? _____

The number of pages read (to the nearest multiple of 50) by the students in Mr. Sullivan's class last week are shown in the tally table at the right.

Pages	Tally
50	I
100	
150	II
200	THH I
250	I
300	THH
350	III
400	IIII
450	I
500	I

3. Find the mean, the median, and the mode of the data.

   _____

4. What is the outlier in this set of data? _____

5. Does the outlier raise or lower the mean? _____

6. Would you use the mean, median, or mode to most accurately reflect the typical number of pages read by a student?

   Explain. _____

   _____

Kenny hopes to have a 9-point average on his math quizzes. His quiz scores are 7, 6, 10, 8, and 9. Each quiz is worth 12 points.

7. What is Kenny's average quiz score?

   _____

8. There are two more quizzes. How many more points does Kenny need to have a 9-point quiz average? _____

9. Write the numbers from 1 to 6 on slips of paper. Place the numbers in a paper bag or an envelope. Draw out a number 20 times, each time replacing the number before drawing again. Complete the tally table. Find the mean, median, and mode.

   _____

   _____

Number	Tally
1	_____
2	_____
3	_____
4	_____
5	_____
6	_____

Activity 1: Choosing an Appropriate Measure

1. Work in a small group. You will be gathering
   information about each member of your group.

   a. With a measuring tape, find the height
      (in centimeters) of each member of your group.

   b. Find your pulse either on your wrist or on your
      neck. Use a watch. Count your pulse for 30 seconds.
      Multiply the count by two to find your pulse rate, the
      number of heartbeats per minute.

   c. Record the age, in months, of each group member.

   d. Record the number of people in each member's family, including
      herself or himself.

   e. Record the eye color of each group member.

   f. Record the hair color of each group member.

   g. Record the number of hours, if any, each group member works
      each week in part-time jobs.

   h. Record one or more additional traits about the members of your group.

Materials
- measuring tape
- watch or clock that measures seconds
- calculator

Use the information your group has gathered to answer each question.

2. For which traits can you find the mean? _____

3. For which traits can you find the mode? _____

4. Find the mean where appropriate, and mode for each trait.

Trait	Mean	Mode
Height		
Pulse rate		
Age		
Family size		

Trait	Mean	Mode
Eye color		
Hair color		
Work hours		
Other		

5. What is the typical member of your group like? _____
   _____

6. Combine your group's information with the information gathered by
   the other groups. Find the class mean and/or mode for each trait.
   Create a student "profile" for your class.

Activity 2: Average Temperature

1. The table at the right shows daily temperatures for two days in a number of the major cities in the United States. Work together in small groups. Make a stem-and-leaf plot for today's high temperatures.

2. Write a one-paragraph description of the information shown in the stem-and-leaf plot. For example, tell which cities have similar temperatures, which ones have the most different temperatures, etc.

3. Determine the measures of central tendency for the set of data. Then tell which city or cities have the mean temperature, which have the median temperature, and which have the mode. In your group discuss which of these measures best reflects the average temperature for this day.

	Yesterday	Today		Yesterday	Today
	Hi/Lo	Hi/Lo		Hi/Lo	Hi/Lo
Albany, NY	79/65	80/64	Juneau, AK	53/47	58/44
Albuquerque, NM	88/55	89/55	Louisville, KY	85/67	85/70
Amarillo, TX	84/59	75/55	Memphis, TN	91/74	88/74
Anchorage, AK	55/46	60/44	Miami Beach, FL	83/78	87/78
Atlanta, GA	92/71	90/71	Nashville, TN	89/69	88/69
Atlantic City, NJ	80/68	77/69	New Orleans, LA	90/72	88/71
Austin, TX	78/67	86/68	New York City, NY	78/69	76/65
Baltimore, MD	87/68	87/68	Omaha, NE	74/61	74/54
Billings, MT	63/43	75/45	Orlando, FL	95/70	91/71
Boise, ID	73/36	85/45	Philadelphia, PA	86/72	86/68
Boston, MA	64/54	63/55	Phoenix, AZ	105/78	107/77
Buffalo, NY	84/63	77/65	Pittsburgh, PA	82/75	80/66
Charleston, WV	85/62	84/67	Portland, ME	63/54	62/53
Cheyenne, WY	69/40	75/39	Portland, OR	78/45	89/50
Chicago, IL	81/66	76/62	Providence, RI	75/67	70/58
Cincinnati, OH	84/65	83/71	Raleigh, NC	91/66	89/66
Cleveland, OH	86/64	82/69	Richmond, VA	87/66	89/67
Columbus, OH	84/63	81/72	St. Louis, MO	90/66	80/68
Denver, CO	77/46	78/46	Salt Lake City, UT	73/45	80/48
Des Moines, IA	75/61	74/52	San Antonio, TX	87/66	89/67
Detroit, MI	82/64	78/66	Seattle, WA	70/48	81/50
El Paso, TX	97/59	96/61	Spokane, WA	67/36	78/42
Fairbanks, AK	66/50	63/50	Syracuse, NY	80/65	79/63
Hartford, CT	81/68	77/60	Topeka, KS	83/65	78/58
Helena, MT	62/42	74/36	Tucson, AZ	100/65	102/67
Honolulu, HI	86/66	86/68	Tulsa, OK	88/73	78/64
Houston, TX	86/73	87/72	Washington, DC	89/68	88/70
Indianapolis, IN	88/67	82/68	Wichita, KS	88/66	79/58

4. Using information from your local newspaper, radio, or television, make a record of the daily high and low temperatures in your area for one month. Also, each day during class, measure and record the temperature outside. When you have gathered the three sets of data for one month, construct three line plots. Show the data using three different colors or three different kinds of lines, such as solid, dotted, and broken lines.

5. How does the plot of the measurements taken during the class period compare with the plots for the highs and lows? Do the class measurements represent the average temperature in your area each day? Explain.

6. Find the mean, median, and mode for each set of data. Which do you think best reflects the daily average temperature? Why?

Activity 3: Wink Count

Work together with three or four other students to do this activity.

1. Each person will wink his or her right eye for one minute. He or she will count the winks and record the result in the following table.

Person	1	2	3	4	5
Winks					

2. Find the measures of central tendency for the data.

   Median = _____   Mean = _____   Mode = _____

3. Which person in your group is closest to having the median?

4. Suppose another person joins your group. How many times would this person have to wink in one minute to raise the mean by 10 winks?

5. Collect the results from all of the other groups in the class. Combine the results and find the measures of central tendency.

   Median = _____   Mean = _____   Mode = _____

6. Now have each person wink his or her left eye. Collect the results from all the groups in the class and fine the measures of central tendency.

   Median = _____   Mean = _____   Mode = _____

   Was there any difference between the figures for the right eye and those for the left eye?

EXTRA Work with your group to solve the following problems.

7. The Dragons, a baseball team, have played 15 games so far this season, averaging 2.8 runs per game. Last season, they averaged 3.0 runs per game. They have 3 games remaining on their schedule. How many runs must they score in these games so that their average for this season will be at least as good as their average for last season? Show three different ways they might score this number of runs in 3 games. How many more ways are there, if any?

Puzzle: Mean, Median, and Mode

Work together in small groups to find the following sets of numbers.

1. Find a set of five nonnegative integers such that their mean is 5, their median is 5, and their mode is 7. _____

2. Collect the solutions to Exercise 1 from all the groups in the class. Do you think that the class has found all of the possible sets of five such integers? Why do you think this? _____

3. How many possible sets of five nonnegative integers will satisfy the conditions given in Exercise 1? Explain how you arrived at your answer and why you think that it is correct. _____

4. What is the probability that the set of five integers that satisfy the conditions in Exercise 1 will contain

    a. one seven? _____   **b.** two sevens? _____   **c.** three sevens? _____

    d. four sevens? _____   **e.** five sevens? _____

For the following exercises, each set of numbers consists of five integers such that $0 \le N \le 20$. Find a set of numbers that satisfies the given conditions. Calculate each measure of central tendency to verify your solution. Be prepared to explain how you found the set.

5. The mean, median, and mode are equal. _____

6. The mean is greater than both the median and the mode.

_____

7. The mean is less than both the median and the mode.

_____

8. The mode is greater than the mean but less than the median.

_____

9. The difference between the mean and the median is greater for this set than for any other possible set. _____

Name _____ Class _____ Date _____

Reteaching: Mean, Median, and Mode

Find the mean, median, and mode of this list of numbers.

32, 33, 41, 29, 41, 39, 30

Mean		**Median**	**Mode**
Add. → 32	**Divide by the number**	29	**41** occurs twice.
33	**of numbers.**	30	
41	↓	List the 32	**Find the most**
29	**35**	numbers → 33	**frequently**
41	7)245	in order. 39 ← Choose	**occurring number.**
39	21	41 **the middle**	
+ 30	35	41 **number**	
245	35		
	0		
Mean = 35		Median = 33	Mode = 41

Find the mean, median, and mode of each list of numbers.

1. 9, 13, 10, 16

Median = _____   Mean = _____   Mode = _____

$9 + 13 + 10 + 16 = 48$ 9, 10, 13, 16

4)48   Average the middle numbers.

$$\frac{10 + 13}{2} = \frac{23}{2}$$

2. 84¢, 85¢, 89¢, 91¢, 86¢, 87¢

Mean = _____

Median = _____

Mode = _____

3. 235, 229, 221, 231, 239

Mean = _____

Median = _____

Mode = _____

4. 43, 36, 43, 65, 49, 53, 61

Mean = _____

Median = _____

Mode = _____

5. $116, $124, $148, $129, $133

Mean = _____

Median = _____

Mode = _____

Assessment 2: Measures of Central Tendency

Seven students were timed as they skied on the same course. Here are their times (in minutes and seconds):
2:03   1:45   1:47   1:51   2:03   1:58   3:03

1. Which of the times is an outlier? _____

2. What is the mean time for all the racers, including the outlier? Without the outlier? Give your answers to the nearest second.

   _____

3. What is the median time? _____

4. What is the mode for this data? _____

5. Which measure of central tendency gives the best sense of the skiers' performance? Why?

   _____

6. Which measure of central tendency gives the poorest sense? Why?

   _____

7. What is the range of this data? What does the range represent in terms of the skiers' performance?

   _____

The average noontime temperature in January in Carla's home town is 40°F. During the first days of January this year, Carla measured the temperatures in the table below.

January day	1	2	3	4	5	6	7	8	9	10
Temperature (°F)	33	34	33	35	35	37	39	43	43	45

8. Is the mean noontime temperature for these days above or below the January average in Carla's town? By how much (to the nearest tenth of a degree)? _____

9. Suppose the noontime temperature is exactly the same on each of the remaining days of the month. To the nearest degree, what would that temperature have to be for the January mean to match the historical average? _____

10. Suppose the noontime temperature is 40° on each of the remaining days of the month except the last day. What would the temperature have to be on the last day of January for the January mean to match the historical average? _____

Choosing an Appropriate Graph

Bar graphs are useful for comparing sets of data.

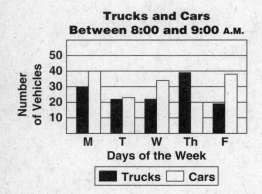

Line graphs and multiple line graphs show how data change over time. Line graphs help you see a trend.

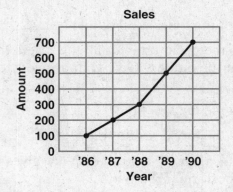

Circle graphs help you see how a total is divided into parts. The parts may represent actual amounts or percents. If the parts represent percents, the entire circle is 100%.

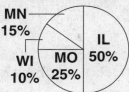

Decide which type of graph is an appropriate display for the data given: *circle graph, line graph, multiple line graph,* **or** *double bar graph.* **Explain your choice.**

1. two classes' test scores over a school year

_____

2. how a club spends its money

_____

3. the numbers of boys and the numbers of girls who use the playground each day for one week

_____

4. the percents of chemical elements in seawater

_____

5. the numbers of store customers per hour in one day

_____

Name _____ Class _____ Date _____

Practice: Choosing an Appropriate Graph

Use the circle graph.

1. From which group are about $\frac{1}{3}$ of used cars purchased?

_____

2. If 49,778 people bought used cars one month, estimate how many bought them from a dealership.

_____

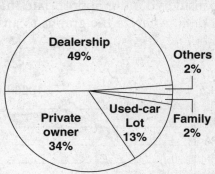

Where Americans Buy Used Cars

Dealership 49%
Others 2%
Private owner 34%
Used-car Lot 13%
Family 2%

Source: *USA Today from Ameripoll, Maritz Marketing Research*

Decide which of the two types of graphs is an appropriate display for the given data. Explain your choice.

3. line graph or circle graph?
sizes of U.S. farms from 1950 to 1990

_____

4. bar graph or scatter plot?
lengths of rivers

_____

5. scatter plot or histogram?
height versus weight of students in a class

_____

6. scatter plot or circle graph?
the way a family budgets its income

_____

_____

Decide which of the two types of graphs is an appropriate display for the given data. Then, make the graph.

7. bar graph or line graph?

_____

U.S. Endangered Animals

Type	Number
Mammals	65
Birds	78
Reptiles	14
Amphibians	12
Fish	71
Snails	21
Crustaceans	18

Activity: Appropriate Graphs

The graphs below are based on identical data. One graph is considered more appropriate than the other for this set of data. Analyze the graphs to answer the questions below.

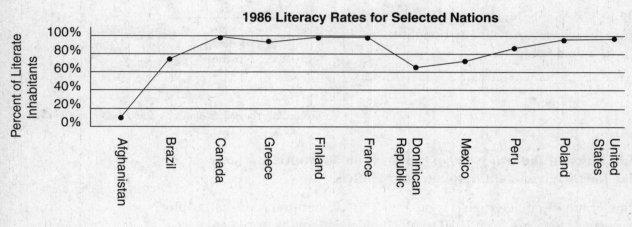

1986 Literacy Rates for Selected Nations

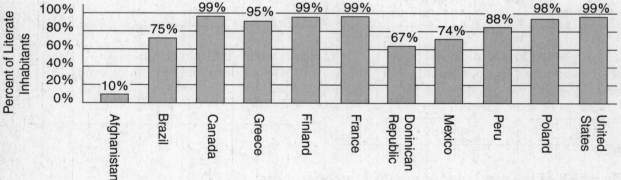

1. Which graph leads you to believe that the literacy rates of the nations listed are related and therefore reflect a trend?

   _____

2. Which graph leads you to believe that the literacy rates of the nations listed are unrelated statistics?

   _____

3. Are the literacy rates of one nation directly related to those of other nations?

   _____

4. Which graph do you feel is more appropriate for the data? Why?

   _____

Misleading Graphs

Data can be displayed on graphs in ways that are misleading.

The horizontal scales make these graphs seem different.

As the numbers are moved farther apart, it appears that the change over time is less.

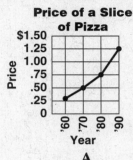

Price of a Slice of Pizza

A

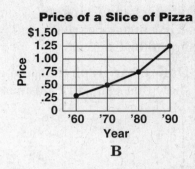

Price of a Slice of Pizza

B

These graphs may seem different because of how the vertical scales are drawn.

The break in the vertical scale makes the differences seem greater than they really are.

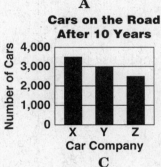

Cars on the Road After 10 Years

C

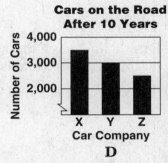

Cars on the Road After 10 Years

D

Use the graphs above to answer Exercises 1–6.

1. Which graph might be used to convince someone that the price of pizza has risen too quickly over the years?

   _____

2. Which graph might be used to convince someone that pizza makers should raise their prices?

   _____

3. Name 2 ways in which the pizza graphs differ.

   _____

   _____

4. Which graph would Car Company X use to show that its cars last longer than the competition?

   _____

5. Which graph of cars still on the road after 10 years would Car Company Z prefer?

   _____

6. Name 2 ways in which graphs C and D differ.

   _____

   _____

Practice: Misleading Graphs

There are only two used car dealers in Auto City, Junkers and Clunkers. Monthly auto sales for January, February, and March are shown for Clunkers.

Clunker's Monthly Auto Sales	
January	15
February	14
March	13

1. Draw a bar graph that Junkers could use to show that Clunkers' business is really falling off.

2. Draw a line graph that Clunkers could use to show that business has been stable.

3. What is the actual decline in auto sales for Clunkers?
   _____

4. Using data from the first three months of the year, can you determine if sales for the whole year will be bad? Explain.
   _____
   _____
   _____

Use the line graph for Exercises 5 and 6.

5. What is wrong with the way the graph is drawn?
   _____
   _____

6. What impression does the graph try to present?
   _____
   _____

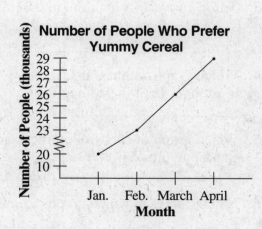

Name _____ Class _____ Date _____

Activity: Analyzing Graphs

Lois and Harold each made an interval graph using the data below.

Years of Service for Teachers in Our School

Mr. Page	1	Ms. Reiner	6	Miss Han	8	Mrs. Kozar	8
Mrs. Green	22	Mr. O'Neil	19	Ms. Burns	5	Mr. Moore	11
Ms. Dean	9	Mr. Garcia	15	Ms. Hinks	6	Miss Parks	7
Mrs. Kanaka	2	Mrs. Judd	15	Mr. Spasky	17	Ms. Diaz	4

1. Finish each graph.

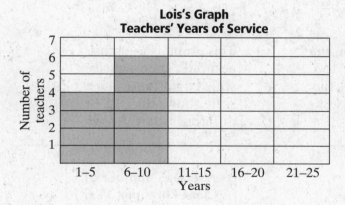

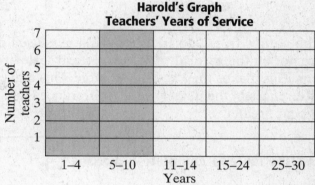

2. How is Lois's graph different from Harold's graph? Which graph gives a more useful picture of the teachers' years of service? _____

_____

_____

3.

NL stock	Week	1	2	3	4	5
	Price	$24.00	$23.25	$23.00	$22.75	$22.00

Use the data in the chart. Draw a graph to support one of these statements:

A. NL stock prices have fallen dramatically over the past 5 weeks.

B. NL stock prices have declined gradually over the past 5 weeks.

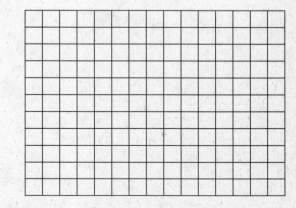

Using Graphs to Persuade 1

The graphs show the same information but give different impressions.

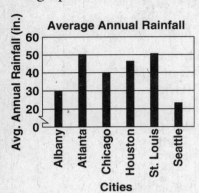

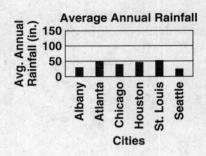

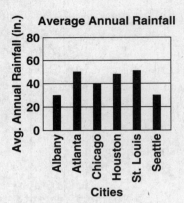

The values from 0 to 10 are not on the vertical axis. This makes the differences in the data appear greater.

Numbers used on the vertical scale are too large. This makes the differences look less significant.

This graph is the most accurate. The vertical scale begins at 0. The scale shows the differences fairly.

Use the table to complete Exercises 1–4.

1. Suppose a bar graph was made using intervals of 100 on the vertical axis. Would the scale show differences in the data fairly? _____

2. Which scale range on the vertical axis would present the data more accurately, 60 to 120 or 0 to 120? _____

3. Draw a graph to make the differences in the data appear unfairly small.

4. Draw a graph that accurately represents the data in the table.

Average Number of Clear Days per Year	
Albany	62
Atlanta	114
Boise	116
Houston	85
St. Louis	80
Seattle	66

Using Graphs to Persuade 2

Use the data in the table. Draw a line graph on each grid at the right. Discuss the impressions given by the graphs.

U.S. Commercial Airline Traffic

Year	1995	1996	1997	1998	1999	2000
Departures (millions)	8.0	8.2	8.1	8.2	8.6	9.0

The first graph gives the impression that airline traffic increased rapidly from 1995 to 2000. The second graph implies a much more gradual increase. The different impressions are given by the vertical scales. The vertical scale in the first graph is broken and increases by half millions. The vertical scale in the second graph is unbroken and increases by three millions.

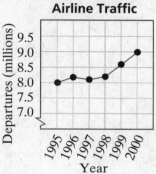

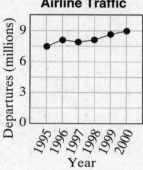

U.S. Average Gasoline Retail Prices

Year	1996	1997	1998	1999	2000	2001
Price (in $)	1.29	1.29	1.12	1.22	1.56	1.53

1. Make a line graph of the data in the table using the grid below.

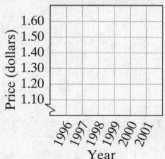

2. Make a line graph of the data in the table using the grid below.

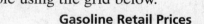
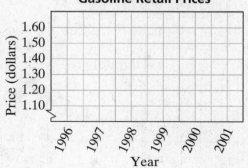

3. Compare the impressions given in the two graphs.

_____

_____

_____

Practice: Using Graphs to Persuade

Use the graph at the right for Exercises 1–5.

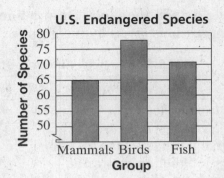

1. Which group of animals appears to have about twice as many endangered species as mammals?

   _____

2. Does one group actually have twice as many endangered species as mammals?

   _____

3. What gives the impression that one group has twice as many endangered species as mammals?

   _____

4. Redraw the graph without a break.

5. Describe the effect the change in scale has on what the graph suggests.

   _____

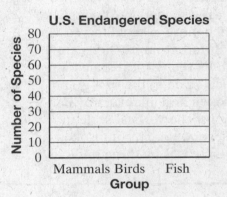

Use the data in the table for Exercises 6–8.

U.S. Union Membership							
Year	1930	1940	1950	1960	1970	1980	1990
Union members (millions)	3	9	14	17	19	20	17

6. Draw a line graph of the data using the grid below.

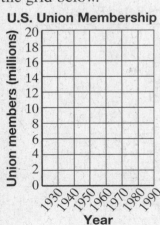

7. Draw a line graph of the data using the grid below.

8. What gives the different impressions in the two graphs?

   _____

Analyzing Games and Making Predictions

A game is **fair** if the players are equally likely to win. Read the rules for the game below. Determine whether the game is fair.

Player A and Player B each toss 2 coins. If there are exactly 2 heads and 2 tails, Player A scores 1 point. Otherwise, Player B scores 1 point. The player with the most points after 10 rounds wins.

Random Number Table			
23948	71477	12573	05954
65628	22310	09311	94864
41261	09943	34078	70481
34831	94515	41490	93312
09802	09770	11258	41139
66068	74522	15522	49227

You can use the random number table above. Read it from left to right. Use 4 digits at a time.

> Let 0, 2, 4, 6, and 8 = head.
> Let 1, 3, 5, 7, and 9 = tail.

The outcomes and winners for the first 10 rounds are:

HTTH	HTTH	TTTH	TTTH	TTTH	HTHH	HHHT	THHT	TTTT	HHHH
A	A	B	B	B	B	B	A	B	B

In 10 rounds, Player A wins 3 points while Player B wins 7. This suggests that A and B are not equally likely to win. The game seems to be unfair.

Solve by simulation or by analyzing the sample space of all possible outcomes for the game above.

1. Suppose you look at only the first 8 rounds using the random number table to simulate the game. Do these results suggest that the game is fair? Explain.

_____

_____

_____

2. Use the random number table. What are the outcomes of rounds 11–20? How many rounds does each player win?

_____

_____

_____

3. Do the random number table results for 20 rounds suggest that the game is fair? Explain.

_____

_____

_____

4. Change the game so that Player A will also win if all heads or all tails are tossed. Will the game be fair? Explain by analyzing the sample space.

_____

_____

_____

Practice: Analyzing Games and Making Predictions

For each game, the winner is the player with the most points after 20 rounds. Decide whether each game is fair.

1. Two number cubes are rolled. Player A subtracts the smaller number from the larger number, Player B divides the smaller by the larger; the smaller result wins a point.

   _____

2. Two number cubes are rolled. Player A adds the two numbers and then multiplies by 2. Player B multiplies the first number by 3 and then adds the second number. The larger result wins a point.

   _____

3. Two number cubes are rolled. The numbers are added. If the sum is even, Player A wins a point. If the sum is odd, Player B wins a point.

   _____

4. Two number cubes are rolled. If the product is odd, Player A wins a point. If the product is even, Player B wins a point.

   _____

Use these random digits in Exercises 5–10.

23948	71477	12573	05954	65628
22310	09311	94864	41261	09943

5. Jason guesses on a multiple-choice test. There are 50 questions, each with 5 possible answers. What digits could you use for a correct guess? What digits could you use for an incorrect guess?

   _____

6. Based on your answer for Exercise 5 and using the random digits, what will Jason's score be?

   _____

   _____

7. If the probability that Julie guesses correctly is 50%, what digits could you use for a correct guess and for an incorrect guess?

   _____

8. Based on your answer for Exercise 7 and using the random digits, what will Julie's score be?

   _____

   _____

9. The probability that Aaron guesses correctly is 80%. What digits could you use for a correct guess and an incorrect guess for Aaron?

   _____

10. Based on your answer for Exercise 9, and using the random digits, what will Aaron's score be?

   _____

   _____

Assessment 3: Use and Misuse of Data Displays

Jose wants to make money mowing lawns this summer. He started in the spring, and mowed two lawns the first week, three the second, and four the week after.

1. Draw a graph that Jose can use to show his parents how hard he is working and how rapidly his business is growing.

2. Using the same data, draw a graph that Jose's parents could use to show that the business is growing very slowly.

3. Graph A and Graph B below show two presentations of the same data. Describe a situation in which you might use Graph A.

   _____

   _____

4. Describe a situation in which you might choose to use Graph B instead.

   _____

   _____

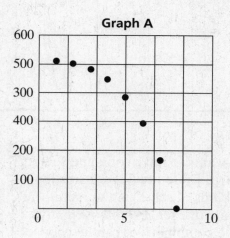

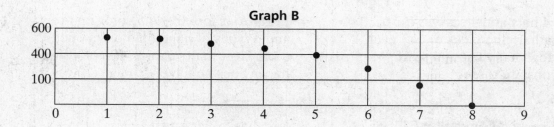

Counting Outcomes

Andy has 3 pairs of pants: 1 gray, 1 blue, and 1 black. He has 2 shirts: 1 white and 1 red. If Andy picks 1 pair of pants and 1 shirt, how many different outfits does he have?

Andy can choose 1 of 3 pairs of pants and 1 of 2 shirts. A tree diagram can help you count his choices.

$$3 \times 2 = 6 \text{ different outfits}$$

The total number of choices is the product of the number of choices for pants and the number of choices for shirts.

You can also use the *counting principle*.

$$n \times m \quad \text{give} \quad n \times m$$

first choices   second choices   total choices

Andy has 6 different outfits.

Find the total number of choices.

1. Moesha has 6 pairs of socks and 2 pairs of sneakers. She chooses 1 pair of socks and 1 pair of sneakers. How many possible combinations are there?

_____

2. Ralph wants to have soup and salad for lunch. There are 5 kinds of soup and 3 kinds of salad on the menu. He picks one of each. From how many possible combinations can he choose?

_____

3. Carla has 4 hats and 4 scarves for winter weather. She picks one of each to wear. How many hat and scarf combinations are there?

_____

4. Lorenzo is looking at 5 color markers and 4 types of paper. He picks one of each. How many choices of color and paper does he have?

_____

5. Eric has 3 baseballs and 4 bats. From how many possible ball and bat combinations can he choose?

_____

6. Kim has 5 swimsuits, 3 pairs of sandals, and 2 beach towels. In how many ways can she pick one of each?

_____

Practice: Counting Outcomes

Draw a tree diagram to show all possibilities.

1. Today, the school's cafeteria is offering a choice of pizza or spaghetti. You can get milk or juice to drink. For dessert you can get pudding or an apple. You must take one of each choice.

2. A clothing store sells shirts in three sizes: small, medium, and large. The shirts come with buttons or with snaps. The colors available are blue or beige.

Choose a calculator, paper and pencil, or mental math.

3. How many license plates are possible if four letters are to be followed by two digits?

_____

4. How many license plates are possible if two letters are to be followed by four digits?

_____

5. A dress pattern offers two styles of skirts, three styles of sleeves, and four different collars. How many different types of dresses are available from one pattern?

_____

6. In a class of 250 eighth graders, 14 are running for president, 12 are running for vice president, 9 are running for secretary, and 13 are running for treasurer. How many different results are possible for the class election?

_____

7. A home alarm system has a 3-digit code that can be used to deactivate the system. If the homeowner forgets the code, how many different codes might the homeowner have to try?

_____

8. A 4-letter password is required to enter a computer file. How many passwords are possible if no letter is repeated and nonsense words are allowed?

_____

Permutations

· ·

The expression 5! is read "5 **factorial**." It means the product of all whole numbers from 5 to 1.

$5! = 5 \cdot 4 \cdot 3 \cdot 2 \cdot 1 = 120$

Evaluate $\frac{5!}{3!}$.

Write the products, then simplify.

$\frac{5!}{3!} = \frac{5 \cdot 4 \cdot 3 \cdot 2 \cdot 1}{3 \cdot 2 \cdot 1} = 5 \cdot 4 = 20$

How many 3-letter codes can be made from A, B, C, D, E, F, G, H with no repeating letters?

This is a **permutation** problem. Order is important. ABC is different from ACB.

- There are 8 choices for the first letter.

- There are 7 choices for the second letter.

- There are 6 choices for the third letter.

The number of codes possible $= 8 \cdot 7 \cdot 6 = 336$.

You can write this as $_8P_3$ meaning the number of permutations of 8 objects chosen 3 at a time.

Evaluate each factorial.

1. 4! _____

2. 3! _____

3. $\frac{4!}{3!}$ _____

4. $\frac{10!}{8!}$ _____

5. $\frac{9!}{9!}$ _____

6. $5! \times 2!$ _____

Find the value of each expression.

7. $_6P_3$ _____

8. $_5P_2$ _____

9. $_{12}P_3$ _____

10. $_4P_4$ _____

11. $_{15}P_2$ _____

12. $_6P_4$ _____

Solve.

13. In how many ways can you pick a football center and quarterback from 6 players who try out?

_____

14. For a meeting agenda, in how many ways can you schedule 3 speakers out of 10 people who would like to speak?

_____

· ·

Practice: Permutations

Use a calculator, paper and pencil, or mental math to evaluate each factorial.

1. 6!

2. 12!

3. 9!

4. $\frac{8!}{5!}$

5. $\frac{12!}{3!}$

6. $_9P_5$

7. $_8P_2$

8. $_{10}P_8$

9. $_5P_5$

10. $_{15}P_6$

Solve.

11. In how many ways can all the letters of the word WORK be arranged?

12. In how many ways can you arrange seven friends in a row for a photo?

13. A disk jockey can play eight songs in one time slot. In how many different orders can the eight songs be played?

14. Melody has nine bowling trophies to arrange in a horizontal line on a shelf. How many arrangements are possible?

15. At a track meet, 42 students entered the 100-m race. In how many ways can first, second, and third places be awarded?

16. In how many ways can a president, a vice president, and a treasurer be chosen from a group of 15 people running for office?

17. A car dealer has 38 used cars to sell. Each day two cars are chosen for advertising specials. One car appears in a television commercial and the other appears in a newspaper advertisement. In how many ways can the two cars be chosen?

18. A bicycle rack outside a classroom has room for six bicycles. In the class, 10 students sometimes ride their bicycles to school. How many different arrangements of bicycles are possible for any given day?

19. A certain type of luggage has room for three initials. How many different 3-letter arrangements of letters are possible?

20. A roller coaster has room for 10 people. The people sit single file, one after the other. How many different arrangements are possible for 10 passengers on the roller coaster?

Combinations
· ·

Mr. Wisniewski wants to pick 2 students from Minh, Joan, Jim, Esperanza, and Tina to demonstrate an experiment. How many different pairs of students can he choose?

In this **combination** problem, the order of the choice of students does not matter. These are the possibilities:

Minh-Esperanza
Minh-Jim   Esperanza-Jim
Minh-Joan   Esperanza-Joan   Jim-Joan
Minh-Tina   Esperanza-Tina   Jim-Tina   Joan-Tina

There are 10 possible combinations.

The number of combinations of 5 students taken 2 at a time is $_5C_2$ where:

$$_5C_2 = \frac{1}{2!}\, _5P_2 = \frac{1}{2!} \cdot 5 \cdot 4 = 10$$

In general,
the number of combinations of n objects taken r at a time is $_nC_r$ where:

$$_nC_r = \frac{1}{r!} \cdot _nP_r$$

Find each number of combinations.

1. $_6C_3$ _____   **2.** $_5C_2$ _____   **3.** $_7C_5$ _____

4. $_4C_3$ _____   **5.** $_8C_2$ _____   **6.** $_6C_4$ _____

7. $_9C_4$ _____   **8.** $_5C_3$ _____   **9.** $_6C_5$ _____

10. $_7C_3$ _____   **11.** $_8C_3$ _____   **12.** $_9C_3$ _____

Find each number of combinations.

13. In how many ways can Susie choose 3 of 10 books to take with her on a trip? _____

14. In how many ways can Rosa select 2 movies to rent out of 6 that she likes? _____

15. In how many ways can Bill pick 2 of his 7 trophies to show his grandfather? _____

16. In how many ways can Mr. Wu choose 5 tulip bulbs out of 15 to plant in a flower bed? _____

17. In how many ways can a town name 5 citizens out of 10 to serve on a committee? _____

18. In how many ways can Mrs. Harris pick 3 flowers from 8 for a bouquet? _____

Practice 1: Combinations

Compute each number of combinations.

1. $_9C_1$

2. $_8C_4$

3. $_{11}C_4$

4. $_{11}C_7$

_____

_____

_____

_____

5. $_4C_4$

6. $_9C_3$

7. $_{12}C_6$

8. $_8C_2$

_____

_____

_____

_____

9. 3 videos from 10 **10.** 2 letters from

_____   LOVE _____

11. 4 books from 8 **12.** 5 people from 7

_____

_____

Solve.

13. Ten students from a class have volunteered to be on a committee to organize a dance. In how many ways can six be chosen for the committee?

_____

14. Twenty-three people try out for extra parts in a play. In how many ways can eight people be chosen to be extras?

_____

15. A team of nine players is to be chosen from 15 available players. In how many ways can this be done?

_____

16. In a talent show, five semi-finalists are chosen from 46 entries. In how many ways can the semi-finalists be chosen?

_____

17. At a party there are 12 people present. The host requests that each person present shake hands exactly once with every other person. How many handshakes are necessary?

_____

18. In math class there are 24 students. The teacher picks 4 students to serve on the bulletin board committee. How many different committees of 4 are possible?

_____

19. Five friends, Billi, Joe, Eduardo, Mari, and Xavier, want one photograph taken of each possible pair of friends. Use B, J, E, M, and X, and list all of the pairs that need to be photographed.

_____

_____

20. Choose A, B, C, or D. Which situation described has $_8C_3$ possible outcomes?

A. Select three letters from 8 to form a 3-letter password.

B. Find the possible ways that first, second, and third prize winners can be selected from 8 contestants.

C. Arrange 8 people in 3 rows.

D. Pick a team of 3 people from 8 players.

Practice 2: Permutations and Combinations

Simplify each expression.

1. $_7P_2$ _____

2. $_7C_2$ _____

3. $_8P_3$ _____

4. $_9P_4$ _____

5. $_3C_2$ _____

6. $_{10}C_4$ _____

7. Art, Becky, Carl, and Denise are lined up to buy tickets.

   a. How many different permutations of the four are possible?

   _____

   b. Suppose Ed was also in line. How many permutations would there be?

   _____

   c. In how many of the permutations of the five is Becky first?

   _____

   d. What is the probability that a permutation of this five chosen at random will have Becky first?

   _____

8. Art, Becky, Carl, Denise, and Ed all want to go to the concert. However, there are only 3 tickets. How many ways can they choose the 3 who get to go to the concert?

_____

9. A combination lock has 36 numbers on it. How many different 3-number combinations are possible if no number may be repeated?

_____

Numbers are to be formed using the digits 1, 2, 3, 4, 5, and 6. No digit may be repeated.

10. How many two-digit numbers can be formed? _____

11. How many three-digit numbers can be formed? _____

12. How many four-digit numbers can be formed? _____

13. How many five-digit numbers can be formed? _____

14. How many six-digit numbers can be formed? _____

Name _____ Class _____ Date _____

Assessment 4: Counting Techniques

There are 7 questions on this page.

1. In how many different ways could they be arranged?

   _____

   _____

2. If one more question were added, how would the number of possible arrangements change?

   _____

   _____

Teams A, B, C, D, E and F are in the semi-final playoffs.

3. How many different matches of one team against another team are possible?

   _____

   _____

4. What are the chances that Team A will be randomly assigned to play Team E in the first playoff round?

   _____

   _____

5. How many different ways can the letters of the word ORDER be arranged?

   _____

   _____

6. Give an example that shows the difference between when you would use $_6C_3$ and when you would use $_6P_3$.

   _____

   _____

7. Arrange the following in order from smallest to largest: $_{24}C_6$, $_{24}P_6$, and $24!$.

   _____

   _____

Theoretical Probability

To find a **theoretical probability,** first list all possible **outcomes.** Then use the formula:

$$P(\text{event}) = \frac{\text{number of favorable outcomes}}{\text{total number of outcomes}}.$$

A letter is selected at random from the letters of the word FLORIDA. What is the probability that the letter is an A?

- There are 7 letters (possible outcomes).

- There is 1 A, which represents a favorable outcome.

$$P(A) = \frac{\text{number of favorable outcomes}}{\text{total number of outcomes}} = \frac{1}{7}$$

The probability that the letter is an A is $\frac{1}{7}$.

Selecting a letter other than A is called *not* A and is the **complement** of the event A. The probabilities of an event and its complement add to 1, or 100%.

What is the probability of the event *not* A?

$$P(A) + P(\text{not A}) = 1$$
$$\tfrac{1}{7} + P(\text{not A}) = 1$$
$$P(\text{not A}) = 1 - \tfrac{1}{7} = \tfrac{6}{7}$$

The probability of the event *not* A

(selecting F, L, O, R, I, or D) is $\frac{6}{7}$.

Use the spinner. Write each probability as a fraction. Then write it as a decimal and a percent.

1. $P(5)$

$\dfrac{\text{number of favorable outcomes}}{\text{total number of outcomes}}$

$= \dfrac{\square}{5}$ _____

2. $P(\text{odd number})$

$\dfrac{\text{number of favorable outcomes}}{\text{total number of outcomes}}$

$= \dfrac{2}{\square}$ _____

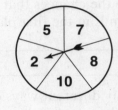

A box contains cards numbered from 1 to 10. Write each probability as a fraction, a decimal, and a percent.

3. $P(\text{even number})$

_____

4. $P(\text{number less than 4})$

_____

5. $P(\text{not 5})$

_____

Use the letters M, A, T, H, E, M, A, T, I, C, and S. Find each probability.

6. $P(M)$ ————

7. $P(\text{not vowel})$ ————

8. $P(\text{not E})$ ————

A number is selected at random from the numbers 1 to 50. Find each probability.

9. $P(\text{multiple of 3})$ ——

10. $P(\text{a factor of 50})$ ——

11. $P(\text{not factor of 50})$ ——

Practice: Theoretical Probability

A spinner numbered 1 through 10 is spun. Each outcome is equally likely. Write each probability as a fraction, decimal, and percent.

1. $P(9)$ **2.** $P(\text{even})$ **3.** $P(\text{number greater than 0})$ **4.** $P(\text{multiple of 4})$

_____   _____   _____   _____

There are eight blue marbles, nine orange marbles, and six yellow marbles in a bag. It is equally likely that any marble is drawn from the bag.

5. Find the probability of drawing a blue marble. _____

6. Find the probability of drawing a yellow marble. _____

7. What marble could you add or remove so that the probability of drawing a blue marble is $\frac{1}{3}$?

_____

Suppose you have a box that contains 12 slips of paper as shown. Each slip of paper is equally likely to be drawn. Find the probability of each event.

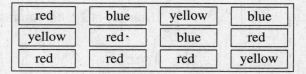

red	blue	yellow	blue
yellow	red ·	blue	red
red	red	red	yellow

8. $P(\text{red})$ **9.** $P(\text{blue})$ **10.** $P(\text{yellow})$

_____   _____   _____

11. $P(\text{red}) + P(\text{blue})$ **12.** $P(\text{red}) + P(\text{yellow})$ **13.** $P(\text{blue}) + P(\text{yellow})$

_____   _____   _____

14. $P(\text{red or blue})$ **15.** $P(\text{red or yellow})$ **16.** $P(\text{blue or yellow})$

_____   _____   _____

17. $P(\text{not red})$ **18.** $P(\text{not blue})$ **19.** $P(\text{not yellow})$

_____   _____   _____

In a raffle, there will be 3 prizes for every 1,000 tickets sold.

20. What is the probability of winning? _____

21. What is the probability of not winning? _____

Name _____ Class _____ Date _____

Reteaching: Theoretical Probability

Spin the spinner.

Chance

There are **3** chances in **8** of stopping on red.

There are **2** chances in **8** of stopping on green.

There are **0** chances in **8** of stopping on yellow.

Probability

➤Probability of red $= \frac{3}{8}$

P(red) $= \frac{3}{8}$

➤P(green) $= \frac{2}{8}$ or $\frac{1}{4}$

➤P(yellow) $= \frac{0}{8}$ or 0

Find each probability.

One of these names is to be drawn from a hat.

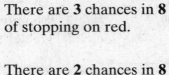

| Mary | Jenny | Bob | Marilyn | Bill | Jack | Jerry | Tina | Connie | Joe |

1. P(3-letter name) $= \dfrac{2}{10}$ or $\dfrac{1}{5}$

↑   Number of 3-letter names

↑ What is the probability of drawing a 3-letter name?

↑ Total number of names

2. P(4-letter name) $= \dfrac{4}{10}$ or $\dfrac{2}{5}$

3. P(name starting with B) $= \dfrac{2}{10}$ or $\dfrac{1}{5}$

4. P(name starting with T) $=$ _____

5. P(7-letter name) $=$ _____

6. P(name starting with S) $=$ _____

7. P(name ending with Y) $=$ _____

One of these cards will be drawn without looking.

| 10 | 4 | 7 | J | S | 9 | 10 | 2 | M | 5 | 4 | J |

8. P(2) $=$ _____ ⬅— number of twos

⬅— total number of cards

9. P(5) $=$ _____

10. P(J) $=$ _____

11. P(a number) $=$ _____

12. P(4) $=$ _____

13. P(T) $=$ _____

14. P(a letter) $=$ _____

Activity: Finding Errors in Statistical Analysis

Find the error, if any, in each exercise. Identify the step(s) in which the error(s) occur. If the exercise is correct, write, "No errors."

1. One number cube is tossed. What is the probability that an even number will be rolled?

   ☐1 $P(\text{even}) = P(2) + P(4) + P(6)$
   ☐2 $\qquad\qquad\quad = 2 + 4 + 6$
   ☐3 $\qquad\qquad\quad = 12$

2. What is the probability of spinning a number less than four or an odd number on a spinner showing the ten whole numbers from 1 to 10?

   ☐1 $P(<4) + P(\text{odd}) = P(1) + P(2) + P(3) + P(1) + P(3) + P(5) + P(7) + (P9)$
   ☐2 $\qquad\qquad\qquad\quad = \frac{1}{10} + \frac{1}{10} + \frac{1}{10} + \frac{1}{10} + \frac{1}{10} + \frac{1}{10} + \frac{1}{10} + \frac{1}{10}$
   ☐3 $\qquad\qquad\qquad\quad = \frac{8}{10}, \text{ or } \frac{4}{5}$

3. Shown below is a stem-and-leaf diagram of the low temperatures, in degrees Fahrenheit, in Dayton, Ohio, for a ten-day period. Construct a histogram.

Stem	Leaf
0	5, 7
1	2, 4, 4, 6
2	8, 8, 8
3	0

   3 | 0 means 30

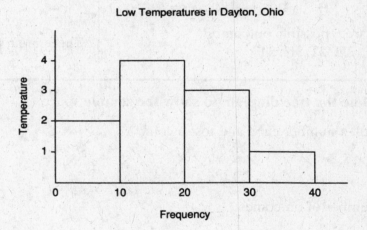

4. Find the mean, median, and mode for the data below.

   1, 7, 6, 8, 7, 4, 2, 5, 9, 12, 3

   ☐1 Mean: The number 7 occurs twice; it is the mean.
   ☐2 Median: The number 4 is the middle number; it is the median.
   ☐3 Mode: There are 11 numbers, and their sum is 64; the mode is $\frac{64}{11}$, or $5\frac{9}{11}$.

Name _____ Class _____ Date _____

Sample Spaces

The set of all possible outcomes of an experiment is called the **sample space.**

You can sometimes use a tree diagram or a table to show the sample space for an experiment. This tree diagram below on the right shows the sample space for spinning the spinner and tossing a coin.

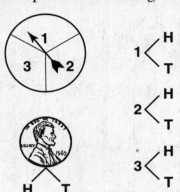

1 < H T

2 < H T

3 < H T

There are 6 possible outcomes:
1H, 1T, 2H, 2T, 3H, 3T

You can use the **counting principle** to find the number of possible outcomes: If there are *m* ways of making one choice and *n* ways of making a second choice, then there are *m* × *n* ways of making the first choice followed by the second.

Evelyn and Kara are planning to go skating or to a movie. Afterward they want to go out for pizza, tacos, or cheeseburgers. How many possible choices do they have?

• There are *two choices* for an activity and *three choices* for food.

• First choices × Second choices

   2   ×   3   = 6

There are 6 possible choices.

Complete the tree diagram to show the sample space.

1. Roll a number cube and toss a coin.

  1   2   3   4   5   6

 Number of outcomes _____

2. Choose the letter *m* or *n* and then choose a vowel.

 Number of outcomes _____

Find the number of possibilities.

3. 4 kinds of yogurt and 8 toppings _____

4. 6 shirts and 9 pairs of slacks _____

5. 3 types of sandwiches and 3 flavors of juice _____

6. 4 types of bread and 6 different sandwich spreads _____

Practice: Sample Spaces

••

Solve the problem.

1. A theater uses a letter to show which row a seat is in, and a number to show the column the seat is in. If there are eight rows and ten columns, make a table to show the sample space for the seats.

A coin is tossed three times.

2. **a.** Draw a tree diagram that shows all the possible outcomes of how the coin will land.

   b. Find the probability that the coin will land heads up all three times or tails up all three times. _____

3. A pizza company makes pizza in three different sizes, small, medium, and large. There are four possible toppings, pepperoni, sausage, green pepper, and mushroom. How many different kinds of pizza with one topping are available? _____

Susan, Joanne, and Diane are triplets. Susan has red, blue, green, and yellow sweaters. Joanne has green, red, purple, and white sweaters. Diane's sweaters are red, blue, purple, and mauve. Each girl has only one sweater of each color, and will pick a sweater to wear at random. Find each probability.

4. P(each girl chooses a different color)
   _____

5. P(each girl chooses the same color)
   _____

6. P(two girls choose the same color, and the third chooses a different color)
   _____

7. P(each girl chooses a red sweater)
   _____

Counting Outcomes and Probability

A basketball team has 2 centers (C1 and C2), 2 point guards (P1 and P2), and 3 shooting guards (S1, S2, S3). Find the sample space and the probability that the first point guard (P1), starts a game if players for the 3 positions are chosen randomly.

You can use a tree diagram to find the sample space.

The tree diagram shows there are 12 possible outcomes. Of the 12 outcomes, 6 include P1:

C1-P1-S1, C1-P1-S2, C1-P1-S3
C2-P1-S1, C2-P1-S2, C2-P1-S3

$P(\text{P1 starts}) = \frac{\text{number of favorable outcomes}}{\text{number of possible outcomes}} = \frac{6}{12} = \frac{1}{2}$

You could also find the number of outcomes in the same space and the favorable outcomes with the Counting Principle.

2 center choices $\times$ 2 point guard choices $\times$ 3 shooting guard choices = 12

There are 12 possible outcomes. The favorable outcomes include 2 choices for center and three choices for shooting guard. However, only one choice for point guard is favorable.

2 center choices $\times$ 1 point guard choice $\times$ 3 shooting guard choices = 6

There are 6 favorable outcomes.

$P(\text{P1 starts}) = \frac{\text{number of favorable outcomes}}{\text{number of possible outcomes}} = \frac{6}{12} = \frac{1}{2}$

A basketball team has 2 centers (C1 and C2), 3 shooting guards (S1, S2, S3), and 3 power forwards (F1, F2, and F3). Players for the 3 positions are chosen randomly to start the game.

1. How many possible outcomes are there in the sample space?

_____

2. List the sample space.

_____

_____

_____

_____

3. Find $P(\text{F2 starts})$. _____   **4.** Find $P(\text{S1 and F1})$ start. _____

Practice: Counting Outcomes and Probability

A computer store sells 4 models of a computer (m1, m2, m3, and m4). Each model can be fitted with 3 sizes of hard drive (A, B, and C).

1. Find the sample space.

_____

_____

2. What is the probability of choosing a computer with a size C hard drive at random?

_____

3. What is the probability of choosing a model 2 computer with a size A hard drive at random?

_____

Solve each problem by drawing a tree diagram.

4. A ballot offered 3 choices for president (A, B, C) and 2 choices for vice president (M, N). How many choices for a combination of the two offices did it offer? List them.

_____

5. The Cougar baseball team has 4 pitchers (P1, P2, P3, P4) and 2 catchers (C1, C2). How many pitcher-catcher combinations are possible? List them.

_____

_____

Solve each problem by using the counting principle.

6. There are 5 roads from Allen to Baker, 7 roads from Baker to Carlson, and 4 roads from Carlson to Dodge. How many different routes from Allen to Dodge by way of Baker and Carlson are possible?

_____

7. Drapery is sold in 4 different fabrics. Each fabric comes in 13 different patterns. Each pattern is offered in 9 different colors. How many fabric-pattern-color combinations are there?

_____

Independent and Dependent Events

There are 3 chips in a bag. You draw 2 chips from the bag.

Experiment 1: Draw one chip, put it back. Draw a chip again.

Draw 2 *is not* affected by draw 1.

Two events are **independent** when the outcome of the second *is not* affected by the outcome of the first.

If *A* and *B* are independent events,
$$P(A \text{ and } B) = P(A) \times P(B).$$

Suppose 2 chips in the bag are red and 1 chip is blue. You draw 1 chip and then put it back before drawing a second chip. Find the probability that the chip color in both draws is red.

$$P(\text{red and red}) = P(\text{red}) \times P(\text{red})$$
$$= \tfrac{2}{3} \times \tfrac{2}{3}$$
$$= \tfrac{4}{9}$$

Experiment 2: Draw one chip. Then, draw another without replacing the first.

Draw 2 *is* affected by draw 1.

Two events are **dependent** when the outcome of the second *is* affected by the outcome of the first.

If *A* and *B* are dependent events,
$$P(A, \text{ then } B) = P(A) \times P(B \text{ after } A).$$

Suppose 2 chips in the bag are red and 1 chip is blue. You draw 1 chip and then another without putting the first chip back. Find the probability that both chips are red.

$$P(\text{red, then red})$$
$$= P(\text{red}) \times P(\text{red after red})$$
$$= \tfrac{2}{3} \times \tfrac{1}{2} = \tfrac{2}{6} = \tfrac{1}{3}$$

A bag has 3 green markers, 3 blue markers, and 2 yellow markers. You randomly choose one marker and then replace it. Then you choose a second marker. Find each probability.

1. $P(\text{green and yellow})$
_____

2. $P(\text{green and blue})$
_____

3. $P(\text{both yellow})$
_____

A drawer has 3 green socks, 4 blue socks, and 2 black socks. You pick one sock at a time and don't replace it. Find each probability.

4. $P(\text{blue, then black})$
_____

5. $P(\text{green, then blue})$
_____

6. $P(\text{black, then green})$
_____

Are the events dependent or independent?

7. flipping a coin twice
_____

8. choosing a hammer and a paint color in a hardware store _____

9. selecting a can of corn and a container of juice in a supermarket
_____

10. picking a board from a pile, nailing it on a fence, then picking another board from the pile _____

Practice 1: Independent and Dependent Events

A shelf holds 3 novels, 2 biographies, and 1 history book. Two students in turn choose a book at random. What is the probability that the students choose each of the following?

1. both novels _____

2. both biographies _____

3. a history, then a novel _____

4. both history books _____

Meg flipped a penny the given number of times. What is the probability the results were as follows?

5. 2; two heads _____

6. 3; three tails _____

7. 2; a tail, then a head _____

8. 5; five tails _____

Two puppies are chosen at random from a box at the mall. What is the probability of these outcomes?

Free Puppies for Adoption!
5 black retrievers
3 brown hounds
4 black setters

9. both black _____

10. both brown _____

11. a setter, then a hound _____

12. a retriever, then a setter _____

13. both setters _____

Are the events independent or dependent? Explain.

14. A guest at a party takes a sandwich from a tray. A second guest then takes a sandwich.

_____

_____

15. Sam flips a coin and gets heads. He flips again and gets tails.

_____

You can select only two cards from the right. Find the probability of selecting a T and an N for each condition.

M A T H
I S
F U N

16. You replace the first card before drawing the second.

_____

17. You do not replace the first card before drawing the second.

_____

Practice 2: Independent and Dependent Events

A bag contains 3 black and 2 white marbles. A marble is drawn at random and then replaced. Find each probability.

1. P(2 blacks) ⸻

2. P(black, white) ⸻

3. P(white, black) ⸻

4. P(2 whites) ⸻

Each letter from the word MISSISSIPPI is written on a separate slip of paper. The 11 slips of paper are placed in a sack and two slips are drawn at random. The first pick is not replaced.

5. Find the probability that the first letter is M and the second letter is I. ⸻

6. Find the probability that the first letter is I and the second letter is P. ⸻

7. Find the probability that the first letter is S and the second letter is also S. ⸻

Solve.

8. On a TV game show, you can win a car by drawing two aces from a standard deck of cards. The first card is not replaced. What is your probability of winning?

   ⸻

9. You roll a number cube eight times, and each time you roll a 4. What is the probability that on the ninth roll, you will roll a 6?

   ⸻

10. Two letters of the alphabet are chosen randomly without replacement. Find each probability.

    a. P(both vowels) ⸻

    b. P(both consonants) ⸻

11. There are 4 brown shoes and 10 black shoes on the floor. Your puppy carries away two shoes and puts one shoe in the trash can and one shoe in the laundry basket.

    a. Complete the tree diagram to show the probability of each outcome.

    b. What is the probability that there will be a brown shoe in both the trash and the laundry basket? ⸻

12. Use the data at the right to find P(right-handed male) and P(left-handed female) if one person is chosen at random.

    ⸻

	Male	Female
Right-handed	86	83
Left-handed	14	17
Total	100	100

Name _____ Class _____ Date _____

Reteaching 1: Independent and Dependent Events

You can select only two cards from the right. Find the probability both are T if you replace the first card before drawing the second and if you do not.

If you replace the first card before drawing the second, then the two events of drawing a card are independent. The first draw *does not* affect the second draw.

Use $P(A \text{ and } B) = P(A) \cdot P(B)$.

$P(\text{T}) = \frac{\text{number of favorable outcomes}}{\text{number of possible outcomes}} = \frac{3}{10}$

$P(2\text{T}) = P(\text{T and T}) = P(\text{T}) \cdot P(\text{T}) = \frac{3}{10} \cdot \frac{3}{10} = \frac{9}{100}$

If you do not replace the first card before drawing the second, the two events of drawing a card are dependent. The first draw *does* affect the second draw.

Use $P(A \text{ and } B) = P(A) \cdot P(B \text{ after } A)$.

For the first draw, $P(\text{T}) = \frac{3}{10}$.

If the card is not replaced, there are only 9 cards left on the second draw.

If a T is drawn the first time and not replaced, there are only 2 T's left on the second draw.

$P(\text{T after T}) = \frac{\text{number of favorable outcomes}}{\text{number of possible outcomes}} = \frac{2}{9}$

$P(2\text{T}) = P(\text{T}) \cdot P(\text{T after T}) = \frac{\cancel{3}}{\cancel{10}_5} \cdot \frac{\cancel{2}}{\cancel{9}_3} = \frac{1}{15}$

So, with replacement, $P(2\text{T}) = \frac{9}{100}$ and, without replacement, $P(2\text{T}) = \frac{1}{15}$.

| S |
| T |
| A |
| T |
| I |
| S |
| T |
| I |
| C |
| S |

You randomly select a card from those above. You replace the card and select a second card. Find the probability of selecting each set of letters.

1. two I's _____

2. S and then I _____

3. C and then T _____

4. T and then S _____

You randomly select a card from those above and, without replacing the card, you select a second card. Find the probability of selecting each set of letters.

5. two I's _____

6. S and then I _____

7. C and then T _____

8. T and then S _____

Analyzing Events Not Equally Likely

The student council president at Whelms Junior High is drawing a name out of a hat to select a council member to represent the student body at a reception for the mayor.

Council Members							
Member	Grade	Member	Grade	Member	Grade	Member	Grade
Dan Jones	8	Jim Monroe	9	Tom Mayer	9	Sue Wiley	9
Mary Mifume	8	Kate Wright	7	Max Doria	9	Judy Stein	8
Joan Carr	7	Jenny Pitt	9	Debbie Lee	7	Mandy Jacobs	7
Miranda Perez	9	Ben Hope	9	Anna Sanchez	8	Russell Young	8
Norm Gant	8	Stew Barns	8	Jack Toth	7	Steve Kasko	9

Complete the frequency chart as needed in order to answer the questions below. Use the probability formula to compute your answers.

1. What is the probability of drawing the name of a council member

   a. who is female? _____

   b. who is male? _____

   c. who is an eighth grader? _____

   d. who is not a seventh grader? _____

   e. who is a ninth grader? _____

   f. who is a male ninth grader? _____

Description	Frequency
female	
male	
eighth grader	

2. What is the probability of drawing the name of either a male or a female? _____

3. The probability of drawing the name of a student who is 14 years old is $\frac{2}{5}$. How many students are 14 years old? _____

4. The probability of drawing the name of a student who has a class with Mr. Cartwright is $\frac{3}{10}$. How many of Mr. Cartwright's students are in the drawing? _____

Practice: Analyzing Events Not Equally Likely

Example   A card is drawn from a well-shuffled deck. What is the probability that the card is a five?

Solution $P(\text{five}) = \frac{4}{52}$ There are 4 fives and 52 possible outcomes.

$= \frac{1}{13}$

A card is drawn from a well-shuffled deck.

1. What is the probability that the card is a nine?   1. _____

2. What is the probability that the card is a six?   2. _____

3. What is the probability that the card is a two?   3. _____

4. What is the probability that the card is a three?   4. _____

5. What is the probability that the card is a four?   5. _____

Suppose you draw 1 card from a standard deck of 52 cards. Find each probability.

6. $P(\text{jack})$ 6. _____

7. $P(\text{red } 10)$ 7. _____

8. $P(\text{club})$ 8. _____

9. $P(\text{not a red card})$ 9. _____

10. $P(\text{face card})$ 10. _____

11. $P(\text{7 of hearts})$ 11. _____

12. $P(\text{not a diamond})$ 12. _____

13. $P(\text{not the ace of spades})$ 13. _____

14. A student reaches into a bag that contains 14 blue pens, 8 black pens, and 6 red pens. What is the probability that the student will pick a black pen?   14. _____

15. Your cousin reaches into a bag that contains 12 popcorn balls, 16 rice cakes, and 10 granola bars. What is the probability that your cousin will pick a rice cake?   15. _____

16. A teacher reaches into a bag that contains 6 plums, 14 clementines, and 12 nectarines. What is the probability that the teacher will pick a clementine?   16. _____

Activity: Analyzing Events Not Equally Likely

Two **complementary** events have probabilities whose sum is 1.

If we have two **mutually exclusive** events A and B, then
$P(A \text{ or } B) = P(A) + P(B)$.

For any two events A and B, $P(A \text{ or } B) = P(A) + P(B) - P(A \cap B)$,
where $A \cap B$ means the intersection of A and B, or A and B both happening.

Examples

An event B has a probability of $\frac{3}{17}$. What is $P(B')$?

Since B and B' are complementary events we know $P(B) + P(B') = 1$.

$\frac{3}{17} + P(B') = 1$ so $P(B') = 1 - \frac{3}{17} = \frac{14}{17}$

A spinner numbered $1-8$ is spun. What is the probability of spinning a 1 or a 5?

Spinning a 1 or a 5 are mutually exclusive events. That is, they cannot occur at
the same time. Thus, $P(1 \text{ or } 5) = P(1) + P(5) = \frac{1}{8} + \frac{1}{8} = \frac{2}{8} = \frac{1}{4}$

A card is drawn from a well shuffled deck of 52 cards. What is the probability of
drawing a diamond or a jack?

Drawing a diamond or drawing a jack are not mutually exclusive events. That
is, they can occur at the same time, namely by drawing the jack of diamonds.

Thus, $P(\text{diamond or jack}) = P(\text{diamond}) + P(\text{jack}) - (\text{diamond} \cap \text{jack})$

$P(\text{diamond}) = \frac{13}{52}, P(\text{jack}) = \frac{4}{52}, P(\text{diamond} \cap \text{jack}) = \frac{1}{52}$

$P(\text{diamond or jack}) = \frac{13}{52} + \frac{4}{52} - \frac{1}{52} = \frac{4}{13}$

---

1. Suppose an event A has a probability of $\frac{3}{7}$. What is $P(A')$? _____

2. Suppose an event AC has a probability of 0.23. What is $P(C')$? _____

3. Suppose that the probability that you will win a contest is 0.0001.
   What is the probability that you will not win the contest? _____

A card is drawn from a well shuffled deck of 52 cards.

4. What is the probability that the card will be a spade or a
   red face card? _____

5. What is the probability that the card will be a red 7 or a
   black face card? _____

6. What is the probability that the card will be even or a
   red card? _____

Activity: Analyzing Theoretical Probability

Directions: Each question or group of questions is based on a given set of conditions. To answer some of the questions it may be useful to make a table or draw a diagram to help you find the answer.

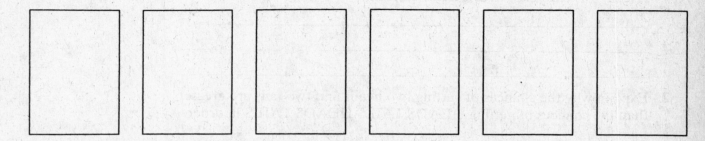

There are 6 index cards lying face down on a table as shown above. Exactly two of these cards have the number 3 written on the hidden side, and you do not know which cards they are. You pick two cards at random.

1. What is the probability that you will pick at least one 3?

2. What is the probability that you will not pick a 3?

3. Are you more likely to pick a 3 or to not pick a 3?

The six faces on a number cube have the numbers from 1 to 6 shown on them. If you roll one number cube, your chance of rolling the number 5 are 1 in 6 or $\frac{1}{6}$. If you roll two number cubes, your chances of rolling a 5 increase. You would think that your chances would be $\frac{1}{6}$ for each number cube, or $\frac{1}{6} + \frac{1}{6}$ or $\frac{1}{3}$ when you roll two. The more number cubes that you roll, the better your chances become. For example, you might think that when you roll six number cubes, your chances of rolling a 5 are $\frac{1}{6} \times 6$, or 1. But a probability of 1 means that you would always roll a 5 when you roll six number cubes. You should know that this is not true. What went wrong?

4. Look over the assumptions that were made to find one or more that were wrong. Then show how or why it or they were wrong.

Assessment 5: Theoretical Probability

You flip a coin four times.

1. Which outcome is more likely: HEADS HEADS HEADS HEADS or HEADS TAILS HEADS TAILS? Explain.

   _____

   _____

   _____

2. Explain why the chances of getting two heads and two tails are greater than the chances of getting HEADS TAILS HEADS TAILS in order.

   _____

   _____

   _____

3. If a family has four daughters in a row, what is the probability that their next child will be a girl too? _____

What are the chances of drawing four aces in a row from a shuffled deck of cards:

4. Without replacement? _____

5. With replacement? _____

6. A good baseball player might bat .333, meaning he gets a hit on average once for every three times at bat. If the player bats three times during a game, what are the chances that he will get at least one hit? _____

7. I have three dress shirts and one tie that goes with each shirt. If I dress in the dark, what are my chances of ending up with a matching shirt and tie? _____

8. The weatherman predicts a 50 percent chance of rain tomorrow and the next day. Merce makes a tree diagram of the weather outcomes for the two days.

   She concludes that the chances of rain on both days is 25%. What is wrong with her analysis?

Theoretical and Experimental Probability

You can collect data through observations or experiments and use the data to state the **experimental probability**.

Alan has a coin. He tosses the coin 100 times and gets 60 heads and 40 tails. The experimental probability of getting heads is:

$$P(\text{heads}) = \frac{\text{number of heads}}{\text{number of trials}} = \frac{60}{100} = 0.6$$

Then Sarita calculated the **theoretical probability** of getting heads on one toss of the coin.

$$P(\text{heads}) = \frac{\text{favorable outcomes}}{\text{number of possible outcomes}} = \frac{1}{2} = 0.5$$

Alan thinks that his coin is unfair since the experimental probability is different from the theoretical probability.

Sarita suggests that they run the experiment again. This time they toss 53 heads and 47 tails. This suggests that the coin is more fair than Alan thinks. To form a more convincing conclusion, they should run the test several more times.

Suppose you have a bag with 75 marbles: 15 red, 5 white, 25 green, 20 black, and 10 blue. You draw a marble, note its color, and then put it back. You do this 75 times with these results: 12 red, 9 white, 27 green, 17 black, and 10 blue. Write each probability as a fraction in simplest form.

	1. $P(\text{red})$	**2.** $P(\text{white})$	**3.** $P(\text{green})$	**4.** $P(\text{black})$	**5.** $P(\text{blue})$
Experimental Probability					
Theoretical Probability					

Suppose you surveyed the students in your class on their favorite juice flavors. Their choices were 6 apple, 10 orange, 1 grapefruit, and 3 mango. Write each probability as a fraction in simplest form.

6. $P(\text{apple})$ **7.** $P(\text{orange})$ **8.** $P(\text{grapefruit})$ **9.** $P(\text{mango})$

_____   _____   _____   _____

Name _____ Class _____ Date _____

Practice: Theoretical and Experimental Probability

A dart is thrown at the game board shown. Find each probability.

1. $P(A)$ _____   **2.** $P(B)$ _____   **3.** $P(C)$ _____

4. $P(\text{not } A)$ _____   **5.** $P(\text{not } B)$ _____   **6.** $P(\text{not } C)$ _____

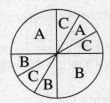

The odds in favor of winning a game are 5 to 9.

7. Find the probability of winning the game. _____

8. Find the probability of *not* winning the game. _____

A bag of uninflated balloons contains 10 red, 12 blue, 15 yellow, and 8 green balloons. A balloon is drawn at random. Find each probability.

9. $P(\text{red})$ _____   **10.** $P(\text{blue})$ _____   **11.** $P(\text{yellow})$ _____ **12.** $P(\text{green})$ _____

13. What are the odds in favor of picking a blue balloon? _____

14. What are the odds in favor of picking a green balloon? _____

15. What is the probability of picking a balloon that is not yellow? _____

16. What is the probability of picking a balloon that is not red? _____

Solve.

17. a. You are given a ticket for the weekly drawing at the grocery store each time you enter the store. Last week you were in the store once. There are 1,200 tickets in the box. Find the probability and the odds of your winning.

_____

b. Find the probability and odds of your winning if you were in the store three times last week and there are 1,200 tickets in the box. _____

18. A cheese tray contains slices of Swiss cheese and cheddar cheese. If you randomly pick a slice of cheese, $P(\text{Swiss}) = 0.45$. Find $P(\text{cheddar})$. If there are 200 slices of cheese, how many slices of Swiss cheese are on the tray? _____

19. For a raffle 10,000 tickets are sold. One ticket is drawn at random to determine a winner. Find the probability and odds of winning. _____

Activity 1: Theoretical and Experimental Probability

1. a. Toss a coin 12 times. Make a check (✓) beside
"Tails" each time a tail appears and beside "Heads"
each time a head appears. To generate the next row,
write the total number of tails (or heads) you have
obtained so far over the number of tosses. Find the
percent by dividing the numerator by the denominator
and rounding to the nearest whole number.

> **Before you begin:** you will
> need a coin.

Tosses	1	2	3	4	5	6	7	8	9	10	11	12
Tails												
Total tails/tosses												
Percent												
Heads												
Total heads/tosses												
Percent												

b. Make a double line graph to show your results. Use
a solid line for the percent of tails obtained. Use a
dotted line for the percent of heads.

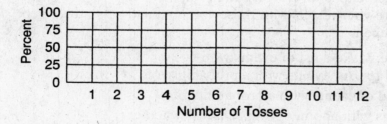

c. Analyze the graph. What do you notice?

_____

_____

_____

_____

Activity 2: Theoretical and Experimental Probability

Work in a small group.

1. Suppose you roll a number cube 12 times. Predict how many times each result in the table at the right will happen. Record your predictions.

2. Now roll a number cube 12 times. Use tally marks to keep a record of what happens.

3. Were all of your predictions correct? _____

4. If you roll a number cube once, what is the probability of rolling a 3? _____

   Did you roll a three exactly one sixth of the time? _____

Result	Prediction	Tally
1		
2		
3		
4		
5		
6		
any number from 1 through 6		
7		

5. Does a probability of $\frac{1}{6}$ for rolling a three mean that you will always roll one three in every six rolls? _____

6. If you answered the above questions "no," then what does a probability of $\frac{1}{6}$ for rolling a three mean? _____

_____

7. Which of the results, if any, were you able to predict exactly? Why?

8. Suppose you had done the experiment for 24 rolls. Do you think the results would have been closer to your predictions? Why or why not?

9. Copy the above table. Make predictions for 24 rolls. Then roll a number cube 24 times. Compare your results with those you obtained for 12 rolls. Discuss what happened.

10. Think of events in everyday life. Make a list of events with a probability of happening equal to 0, of events with a probability of happening equal to *about* $\frac{1}{2}$, and of events with a probability of happening equal to 1. Trade lists with another group. Discuss whether the probabilities on the other group's list are reasonable.

Activity 3: Increasing the Number of Trials

You and a partner can conduct a probability experiment to approximate the value of π. First, recall this definition: Two numbers are *relatively prime* if their only common factor is 1.

Each partner should choose a 2-digit number at random from a phone book or the page numbers of a book. Record the numbers as Trial 1. Conduct as many trials as possible. The more pairs you choose, the closer will be your approximation to π.

Trial	First number	Second number
1		
2		
3		
4		
5		
6		
7		
8		
9		
10		
11		
12		
13		
14		
15		
16		
17		
18		
19		
20		

Trial	First number	Second number
21		
22		
23		
24		
25		
26		
27		
28		
29		
30		
31		
32		
33		
34		
35		
36		
37		
38		
39		
40		

Now find the following.

1. number of trials (N) _____

2. number of relatively prime pairs (R)

   _____

3. To approximate π, find $\sqrt{\frac{6N}{R}}$ using your calculator.

   _____

4. To the nearest thousandth, how far off is your approximation? Use $\pi = 3.142$.

   _____

Predictions Based on Experimental Probabilities

A bottling company puts apple juice into plastic bottles. Each bottle is supposed to have 8 ounces of juice. If bottles have too much juice, the company loses money. If they have too little, consumers may not purchase the product. The quality control department cannot inspect all of the bottles, so it looks at a few from each batch.

A worker inspects 400 bottles. Eight are improperly filled. Based on these data, what is the probability that a randomly chosen bottle has too much or too little juice?

Find the experimental probability:

P(improper fill)

$$= \frac{\text{number of bottles improperly filled}}{\text{total number inspected}}$$

$$= \frac{8}{400} = 0.02$$

The probability is 0.02 or 2%.

If the company produces 15,000 bottles of juice each week, predict the number of bottles that will be improperly filled.

Use the probability

$$P(\text{improper fill}) = 0.02$$
to predict the number.

$$0.02 \times 15{,}000 = 300$$

About 300 bottles will be improperly filled.

Solve. Show your work.

1. The Rainbow Crayon Company ships crayons in large boxes to other companies for packaging. The crayons in each box should not be broken. The quality control department cannot inspect all of the crayons, so it examines a few boxes from each shipment. A worker inspects 600 crayons. Twenty-four are broken. Based on these data, what is the probability that a randomly chosen crayon is broken?

   _____

2. The Rainbow Crayon Company adjusts its packaging. When 500 crayons are inspected, eight are found broken. Has the probability of a broken crayon changed? Explain.

   _____

3. The Rainbow Crayon Company ships 18,000 crayons each week. Predict the number of broken crayons that would be shipped with the old packaging.

   _____

4. Predict the number of broken crayons that would be shipped each week with the new packaging.

   _____

5. What is the probability with the new shipping that a crayon will not be broken?

   _____

Practice: Predictions Based on Experimental Probabilities

Find each answer.

1. A bakery inspects a sample of 800 pastries and finds that 12 are defective. Based on these data, what is the probability that a pastry is defective?

   _____

2. After altering some machinery, the bakery inspects a new sample of 1,500 pastries and finds that 16 are defective. Did quality improve? Explain.

   _____

   _____

Refer to the chart for Exercises 3–6.

Process Control Chart for Defective Pastry

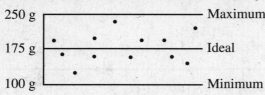

3. What is the ideal weight of a pastry?

   _____

4. What are the maximum and minimum acceptable weights of a pastry?

   _____

5. What is the range of acceptable values?

   _____

6. What does the range tell you?

   _____

   _____

Make a prediction.

7. A car rental agency rented 343 cars last week. Out of those cars, 3 were returned because of mechanical problems. Predict how many cars will be returned for mechanical problems out of 10,000 rentals.

   _____

8. A roller bearing manufacturer found 4 defective roller bearings out of a sample of 500 bearings. Based on this sample, predict how many defective bearings could be expected out of 1,000,000 bearings.

   _____

Reteaching: Predictions Based on Experimental Probabilities

From 8,000 sports shirts produced, a manufacturer takes several random samples. Use the data in the table to estimate the total number of defective shirts based on Sample A.

Sample	Number Sampled	Number Defective
A	250	6
B	400	8
C	500	9

Set up a proportion.

$$\frac{\text{defective sample shirts}}{\text{sample shirts}} = \frac{\text{defective shirts}}{\text{shirts produced}}$$

$\frac{6}{250} = \frac{x}{8,000}$ Substitute.

$250x = 6(8,000)$ Find cross products.

$250x = 48,000$ Simplify.

$\frac{250x}{250} = \frac{48,000}{250}$ Divide each side by 250.

$x = 192$ Simplify.

The total number of defective shirts based on Sample A is about 192.

Use the data in the table above to estimate the number of defective shirts out of 8,000 based on each sample.

1. Sample B _____ proportion used: _____

2. Sample C _____ proportion used: _____

From 12,000 computer games produced, a manufacturer takes several random samples. Use the data in the table to estimate the total number of defective games based on each sample.

3. Sample A _____

   proportion: _____

Sample	Number Sampled	Number Defective
A	400	16
B	800	30
C	500	19

4. Sample B _____

   proportion: _____

5. Sample C _____

   proportion: _____

6. All 3 samples combined _____

   proportion: _____

Assessment 6: Experimental Probability

1. Students sell 300 tickets to the class lottery. If you buy three tickets, what is the probability of winning. What are the odds of your winning?

A bag of change contains 15 quarters, 10 dimes, 12 nickels, and 3 pennies. Students drew out 40 coins at random (with replacement) and got these results: 16 quarters, 9 dimes, 10 nickels, and 5 pennies. Fill in the table below with each probability as a fraction in simplest form.

		Theoretical Probability	Experimental Probability
2.	P (quarter)	■	■
3.	P (dime)	■	■
4.	P (nickel)	■	■
5.	P (penny)	■	■

A CD manufacturer inspects a sample of 200 CDs and finds that 20 are defective.

6. Based on these data, what is the probability that a CD is defective?

   _____

7. Based on this sample, predict how many defective CDs could be expected out of a production run of 1,000,000 disks.

   _____

8. If the CD company wanted a defect rate of less than 5%, how many defective CDs can there be in a sample of 200 disks?

   _____

9. A sample of 25 students contains 1 student over 6 feet tall. Use a proportion to estimate the number of students over 6 feet tall in a junior high school of 500 students.

   _____

Random Samples and Biased Questions

Carlos is curious about sports that students in his school like best. He cannot interview every student in the school. But he could interview a sample of the school **population.**

Carlos wants a **random sample.** A sample is random if everyone has an equal chance of being selected. How will Carlos get a random sample? He considers two possibilities:
① He can interview 30 students at a soccer game.
② He can interview 5 students in each of 6 class changes.

Carlos realizes that students at a soccer game probably like soccer better than other sports. That would not be a random sample. He decides on the interviews during class changes.

What question will he ask? He considers two possibilities:
① "Which sport do you prefer, football, soccer, baseball, or tennis?"
② "Which do you enjoy most, the slow sport of baseball or one of the more exciting sports like football, soccer, or tennis?"

The second question is **biased.** It makes one answer seem better than another. Carlos decides to ask the first question.

Circle the letter of the best answer for Exercises 1 and 2.

1. You want to find how many people in your community are vegetarian. Where would be the best place to take a survey?

   A. a health food store   **B.** a steak house   **C.** a shopping mall

2. Which of these is an unbiased question?

   A. Will you vote for the young inexperienced candidate, Mr. Soong, or the experienced candidate, Ms. Lopez?

   B. Will you vote for Mr. Soong or Ms. Lopez?

You plan to survey people to see what percent own their home and what percent rent. Tell whether the following will give a random sample. Justify your answer.

3. You interview people outside a pool supply store in the suburbs.

   _____

4. You interview people in the street near an apartment complex.

   _____

5. You mail a survey to every 20th person in the telephone book.

   _____

Practice: Random Samples and Biased Questions

You want to survey students in your school about their exercise habits. Tell whether the following will give you a random sample. Justify your answer.

1. You select every tenth student on an alphabetical list of the students in your school. You survey the selected students in their first-period classes.

_____

_____

2. At lunchtime you stand by a vending machine. You survey every student who buys something from the vending machine.

_____

_____

Tell whether the following questions are biased or fair. Rewrite biased questions as fair questions.

3. Do you think bike helmets should be mandatory for all bike riders? _____

4. Do you prefer the natural beauty of hardwood floors in your home? _____

5. Do you exercise regularly? _____

6. Do you eat at least the recommended number of servings of fruits and vegetables to ensure a healthy and long life?

_____

7. Do you prefer the look and feel of thick lush carpeting in your living room? _____

8. Do you take a daily multiple vitamin to supplement your diet?

_____

9. Do you read the newspaper to be informed about world events?

_____

10. Do you feel that the TV news is a sensational portrayal of life's problems? _____

Planning a Survey

· ·

In a survey, the entire group is called the **population.**
A **sample** is a small part of the population.

For a sample to be fair, it should be **random.** In a random sample,
each member of the population has an equal chance of being selected.

- Survey questions can be either
  closed-option or open-option.

  Closed-option questions limit your
  choices. *Example:* Is adventure or
  biography your favorite type of book?

  Open-option questions allow you to
  answer freely. *Example:* What types of
  books do you like to read?

- Survey questions should be fair, not
  biased. They should not make one
  answer appear better than another.

  Biased question: Did you hate that
  movie as much as I did?

  Fair question: What did you think of
  that movie?

**Suppose you want to find out how students feel about new school
colors. Tell whether each survey describes a good sample. Justify
your answer.**

1. You interview students while they
   are in art class.

   _____

   _____

   _____

2. You randomly select students from
   each homeroom in the school.

   _____

   _____

   _____

**Describe each question as *closed-option* or *open-option.*
Then rewrite it in the other form.**

3. Do you think basketball, football,
   hockey, or baseball is most exciting?

   _____

   _____

4. What do you think of the book we just
   finished in English class?

   _____

   _____

Explain why each question is biased.

5. Don't you agree that Mrs. Meredith
   expects too much of her students?

   _____

   _____

6. Were you able to follow that boring
   movie?

   _____

   _____

Name _____ Class _____ Date _____

Practice 1: Planning a Survey

1. What population does the sample represent?

   _____

   _____

In a mall, 2,146 shoppers (age 16 and older) were asked, "How often do you buy shoe polish?" Here is how they responded.

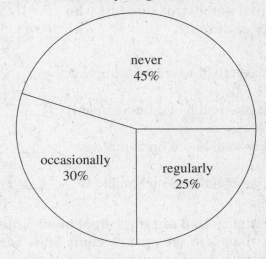

2. How many people responded in each of the categories?

   _____

   _____

3. What is the sample size?

   _____

4. Can you tell if the sample is random?

   _____

5. Is the question open-option or closed-option?

   _____

Explain why the survey questions in Exercises 6 and 7 are biased.

6. Would you rather buy the TV dinner with a picture of a luscious, gourmet meal on it, or one in a plain package?

   _____

   _____

7. Do you want your kids to receive a faulty education by having their school day shortened?

   _____

8. A researcher wants to find out what brand of tomato sauce is most popular with people who work full-time. He samples shoppers at a supermarket between 10 A.M. and 2 P.M. Is this a good sample? Explain.

   _____

   _____

9. You decide to run for student council. What factors are important to consider if you decide to survey your fellow students?

   _____

   _____

Practice 2: Random Samples and Surveys

A school has 800 students. Two random surveys are conducted to determine students' favorite sport. Use the data in the table to estimate the total number of students who prefer each sport.

Sport Samples				
Sample	Number Sampled	Favorite sport		
		Basketball	Football	Baseball
A	40	16	14	10
B	50	22	16	12

1. basketball based on Sample A   _____

2. basketball based on Sample B   _____

3. baseball based on Sample A   _____

4. baseball based on Sample B   _____

You want to find out if a school bond issue for a new computer center is likely to pass in the next election. State whether each survey plan describes a good sample. Explain your reasoning.

5. You interview people coming out of a computer store in your town.

   _____

   _____

   _____

6. You choose people to interview at random from the city telephone book.

   _____

   _____

   _____

7. You interview every tenth person leaving each voting place in your school district.

   _____

   _____

Conducting a Statistical Investigation

The Fun City Magazine Company randomly places one of nine different Fun Stickers in each copy of its magazine. How many copies of the magazine do you think you would have to buy in order to obtain all nine stickers?

Kinds of Stickers

C = Cartoon sticker	N = Nature sticker	F = Friendship sticker
A = Animal sticker	O = Ocean sticker	W = Water sticker
S = Star sticker	H = School sticker	M = Mountain sticker

The table below shows the results of 10 trials. A trial ends when you have at least one of each kind of sticker. The numbers represent the numbers of copies of the magazine with each kind of sticker.

Trial	C	N	F	A	O	W	S	H	M	Total
1	1	5	7	3	2	2	4	7	8	39
2	3	2	1	2	7	3	6	6	2	32
3	1	2	3	2	3	2	7	6	7	33
4	3	2	2	3	1	3	3	4	8	29
5	3	3	8	4	3	1	1	3	2	29
6	2	2	1	3	2	2	2	1	5	20
7	1	3	3	5	1	2	3	4	7	29
8	3	2	2	4	3	1	8	6	5	34
9	2	3	5	4	4	1	3	8	5	25
10	2	3	1	3	1	3	2	6	7	28
										298

From this experiment, the number of copies of the magazine that you would expect you must buy in order to get all nine stickers is given by the following:

$$\text{expected number} = \frac{\text{total number of copies}}{\text{number of trials}}$$
$$= \frac{298}{10}$$
$$= 29.8$$

You would expect that you would have to buy about 30 copies of the magazine in order to get all nine stickers.

Conduct a similar experiment by finding and using your own sample data. Examples of experiments could include the following.

A. How many people in a crowd do you expect to have blue eyes?

B. Out of all the cars that pass a given spot during a certain period of time, how many do you expect to be red?

C. How many people in a group do you expect to tell you that green is their favorite color?

Activity 1: Happy Birthday

What do you think the probability is that two people in your class have the same birthday?

Take a survey of your class and record the results in the table below. For example, if someone's birthday is March 4, record a 4 in the column for March.

Jan	Feb	Mar	Apr	May	Jun	Jul	Aug	Sep	Oct	Nov	Dec

Did at least two people share the same birthday?

According to the results of your survey, what is the probability that

1. someone has a birthday in January?

2. someone has a birthday before June?

3. someone has a birthday on June 24?

4. someone has a birthday on February 29?

5. someone has a birthday in a month with 30 days?

6. someone has a birthday in a month that begins with an A?

Make up a probability question of your own that can be answered by using the data in your survey.

EXTRA: Did you know that two Presidents of the United States had the same birthday? Who were they?

Did you know that three Presidents of the United States died on July 4th? Who were they?

Name ______________________ Class ______________ Date __________

Investigation 2: Hits and Misses (Geometric Probability)

Imagine tossing a penny onto $\frac{3}{4}$-inch graph paper like that shown below in Figure 1. If the penny covers a point of intersection, then the outcome is a "hit." Otherwise, it is a "miss."

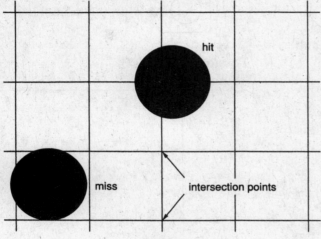

Figure 1

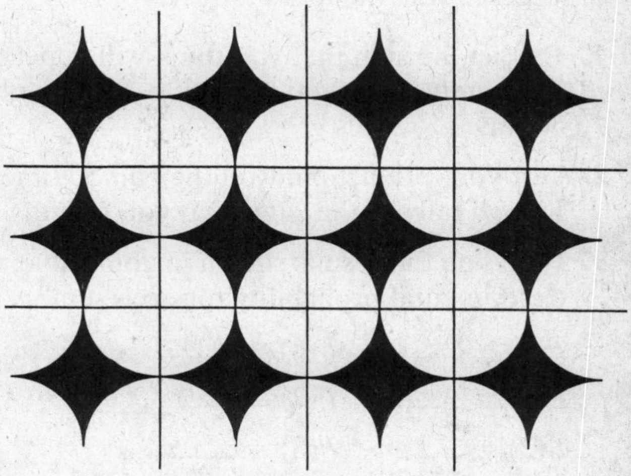

Figure 2

Look at Figure 2. If the center of the coin falls inside a white circle, then the coin will cover an intersection. If the center of the coin falls in a shaded area, then the coin will not cover an intersection.

1. What formula would you use to find the area of each circle in which the center of the coin must fall in order to produce a hit?
2. What is the area of each square in terms of *r*, the radius of each white circle?
3. Write the probability of a hit as a ratio of the area of a white circle to the area of a square. Simplify, if possible.
4. Using 3.14 as an approximation for π, write a decimal for the probability of a hit.

Toss a penny on the graph 100 times. Tally the hits and misses.

Hits— ______________________

Misses—

5. What is the ratio of hits to tosses?
6. Does the data match the expected results?

Perform the experiment again. Combine the results with the results of your first experiment.

7. What is the ratio of hits to tosses?
8. Does the data come closer to matching the expected results?

Activity 3: Sticky-Dot Number Cubes (Theoretical and Experimental Probability)

Take one die of a pair of number cubes and place a sticky dot over the face with six pips. Take the other number cube and place a sticky dot over the face with three pips. Let each sticky dot represent the number 0.

1. Predict the sum that you think will appear most frequently when you roll this pair of number cubes 50 times.

2. Test your prediction. Roll the pair 50 times. Keep a tally of the sums that you rolled.

3. Based on the results shown in your table, what is the experimental probability for each sum?

Possible Sums	Tally
0	
1	
2	
3	
4	
5	
6	
7	
8	
9	
10	
11	

$P(0) =$ _____ $P(6) =$ _____

$P(1) =$ _____ $P(7) =$ _____

$P(2) =$ _____ $P(8) =$ _____

$P(3) =$ _____ $P(9) =$ _____

$P(4) =$ _____ $P(10) =$ _____

$P(5) =$ _____ $P(11) =$ _____

4. Work together in groups of four. Take each of your results from the preceding experiment and combine them. Record the total number of rolls for each possible sum in the table below.

Possible sums	0	1	2	3	4	5	6	7	8	9	10	11
Total rolls												

5. Using the results of your group, calculate the experimental probability for the possible sums.

$P(0) =$ _____ $P(3) =$ _____ $P(6) =$ _____ $P(9) =$ _____

$P(1) =$ _____ $P(4) =$ _____ $P(7) =$ _____ $P(10) =$ _____

$P(2) =$ _____ $P(5) =$ _____ $P(8) =$ _____ $P(11) =$ _____

Compare these experimental probabilities with those you found using the data collected on your own. (See Exercise 3.)

6. Make a table or draw a tree diagram to help you calculate the theoretical probability for each possible sum. Then compare the theoretical probabilities with the experimental probabilities for your group. How close are they? Do you think that combining your group's results with other groups will change this comparison? Explain.

Planning a Simulation

Sometimes it is not reasonable to conduct an experiment in order to determine the probability of an event. In such cases it may be necessary to simulate the event to find the desired probability. To simulate an event, we select an appropriate model that acts out the experiment, and define a trial. Then data can be collected by running a sufficient number of trials.

Example   What is the probability that in a litter of five puppies there will be two male puppies and three female puppies?

Since we are dealing with two possibilities, male or female, we can simulate the situation with a coin toss. Let a head stand for a male puppy and a tail stand for a female puppy. A trial would be a set of five tosses or a toss of five coins.

What is the probability that a family with three children will have exactly one girl?

1. What are you being asked to find?

_____

2. What model can you use to simulate the event?

_____

3. Define a trial for the simulation.

_____

A golf tee manufacturer distributes sample packets containing 6 tees. Each packet contains red, white, and blue tees, with each color equally likely to be included. What is the probability that a packet contains 2 red, 2 white, and 2 blue tees?

4. What are you being asked to find?

_____

5. What model can you use to simulate the event?

_____

6. Define a trial for the simulation.

_____

A garden shop offers packs of one dozen marigold plants. The color of the marigolds in the packs can be gold, bright yellow, or yellow and red, with each color equally likely. What is the probability of buying a market pack that contains exactly four of each color?

7. What model can you use to simulate the event?

_____

8. Define a trial for the simulation.

_____

Simulation 1: A Multiple Choice Test

You can use number cubes to simulate events with random outcomes.

A friend took a five-question multiple-choice test without having studied and answered the questions randomly. Each question had 3 choices. What is the probability that he got 3 or more correct?

You can simulate the situation using five number cubes. Since there are 3 choices for each question but only one correct answer, let 1 or 2 represent the correct answer, 3 or 4 represent one incorrect answer, and 5 or 6 represent the other incorrect answer.

Group each roll (the order of the numbers does not matter), and count the rolls that contain 3 or more digits that are either 1 or 2.

A sample trial of 40 rolls of the five number cubes is shown below.

22245	54411	21524	44632	41464	12614	16656	11465
51365	12535	65622	45361	54125	46432	36321	32216
64131	35463	36252	64132	12514	51351	16566	13561
43221	26532	55562	53455	42345	52364	26261	26626
34635	22326	25431	56552	45235	21344	24344	25155

In this experiment, the eight boxed rolls contain 3 or more 1's and/or 2's.

1. Based on the trial above, what is the probability of getting at least 3 questions correct on the five-question test? _____

2. Perform your own trial of this simulation. How many of your rolls contain 3 or more 1's and/or 2's? _____

3. Based on your trial, what is the probability of getting at least 3 questions correct on the test? _____

4. Suppose the test was a true–false test. Let 1, 2, or 3 represent a correct answer, and 4, 5, or 6 stand for an incorrect answer. Perform a trial of 40 rolls and show the results as above.

5. Count the number of rolls that contain 3 or more numbers that are 1, 2, or 3. _____

6. Based on your trial, what is the probability of getting 3 or more questions correct on a five-question true–false test? _____

7. Count the number of rolls in your trial that contain 4 or more numbers that are 1, 2, or 3. _____

8. From your answer to Question 7, what is the probability that when 5 number cubes are rolled, 4 or more will show 1, 2, or 3?
   _____

9. What does this probability represent, in terms of the true–false test?
   _____

Simulation 2: Dyeing T-shirts

In this activity you use counters to simulate this situation: A shirt manufacturer uses 4 colors, red, green, blue, and yellow, to dye shirts. To dye each shirt, a machine chooses 3 of these colors at random, with possible repetition.

To simulate making 30 shirts, put four counters—one red, one green, one blue, one yellow—in a bag. For each shirt draw out 3 counters, *one at a time, putting each counter back in the bag after it is drawn.* A sample trial of 30 selections of 3 colors each is shown below.

YGY	BGG	YBG	YBR	GBG	YGY
RRR	BYY	RYG	YBG	BRG	BBB
YGR	BYR	GRB	GGR	YYG	BRY
GBR	RRY	RRY	BRR	GYY	YYG
BYG	GRR	BBY	RYB	RGR	BBY

The manufacturer wants to know how many shirts will have three different colors. For this trial, these are boxed in the table.

1. In this trial, how many shirts have 3 different colors? _____

2. From your answer to Question 1, what is probability that a given shirt will have 3 different colors? _____

3. In the trial above, how many shirts have two or more colors that are the same? _____

4. From your answer to Question 3, what is the probability that a shirt will have two or more colors that are the same? _____

5. Do a trial of the simulation above. Write your results in a table like the one above. How many of the "shirts" have 3 different colors? _____

6. According to your trial, what is the probability that a shirt will have 3 different colors? _____

7. How many of the shirts in your trial have two or more colors that are the same? _____

8. According to your trial, what is the probability that a shirt will have two or more colors that are the same? _____

9. Suppose the manufacturer wants to know the probability that all three colors used for a given shirt will be the same. How many times does this happen in the table above? _____ How many times does it happen for your trial? _____

10. What is the probability that all three colors used for a shirt are the same, according to the table above? _____ According to your trial? _____

Simulation 3: Fair Game?

In a fair game involving two players, the probability of winning is $\frac{1}{2}$. This means that in 100 games, you are likely to win 50 times. Try the two games below. For each game, decide if the chances of winning are closer to $\frac{1}{2}$, $\frac{1}{3}$, or $\frac{1}{4}$ in 100 games.

Each game uses four small cards (or pieces of paper) that are exactly alike. Draw a red "X" on 2 of the cards and a blue "X" on the other 2. Place all 4 cards in a paper bag.

For each game, predict player A's chances to win. Then play each game 100 times, and record your results.

Game 1

• Player A, without looking, reaches into the bag and draws a card.

• Player B, also without looking, then draws a card from those remaining.

• If the colors match, player A scores 1 point. Otherwise, player B scores 1 point.

• Return both cards to the bag and mix them thoroughly.

Prediction: _____

Match	
No match	

Game 2

• Player A, without looking, draws a card, reads the color, and returns the card to the bag.

• Player B, also without looking, then draws a card.

• If the colors match, player A scores 1 point. Otherwise, player B scores 1 point.

• Return both cards to the bag and mix them thoroughly.

Prediction: _____

Match	
No match	

1. For each game, do your experimental results support your predictions?

   _____

2. What do you think are the probabilities for matching in each game?

   _____

Analyzing Simulations

1. If you try an experiment n times and you find that m of these are successful, then the probability of success in this experiment is _____.

2. If a thumbtack is tossed 40 times and lands point down 32 times, what is the probability that the thumbtack will land point down? _____

3. Based on the results described in Question 2, what is the probability that the thumbtack will land head down? _____

4. In any sequence of trials of an experiment, what is the sum of the probability of success and the probability of failure? _____

A toothpaste manufacturer took a survey of the popularity of its four flavors of toothpaste: peppermint, spearmint, wintergreen, and cinnamon. The survey polled 40 people, and the probability that any given person would like any given flavor was $\frac{1}{2}$. We can simulate this situation with groups of four coin tosses, heads representing a favorable opinion of a flavor, and tails representing an unfavorable opinion. The results of a 40-trial simulation is shown below. Each block represents the answers of one surveyed person.

```
HHHT   THTT   TTHT   THHT   HHHH   TTHT   HHHT   HHTH
HHHH   THHH   HTHH   TTTH   HHTT   HHTH   HHTH   HTTT
HHTH   TTHT   THTT   THHT   TTHT   HTTH   THHT   TTHH
HTTH   TTTH   TTTT   HHTH   TTTT   TTHT   HHHH   TTTT
HTHH   THTT   HHTT   HTHH   HTHH   TTTT   HHTH   TTHT
```

5. How many of the people surveyed liked three or more flavors? _____

6. Based on your answer to Question 5, what is the probability that a given person would like three or more flavors? _____

7. How many of the people polled in the survey liked two or more flavors? _____ How many liked fewer than two flavors? _____

8. According to the simulation, what is the probability that a given person will like two or more flavors? _____ What is the probability that a person will like fewer than two flavors? _____

9. According to the simulation, what is the probability that a person will like all the flavors of toothpaste? _____

10. Each time you toss a coin, what is the probability of it turning up heads? _____

11. Suppose you wanted to simulate what would happen if 100 people bought state lottery tickets, and suppose you tossed a coin 100 times, with heads representing winning, and tails representing not winning, the lottery. Would you expect an accurate estimate of the probability of winning? _____ Why or why not? _____

Reteaching 1: Simulations

You can use simulation to estimate solutions to probability problems.

A juice company puts one of the five letters, J, U, I, C, and E, inside
the bottle cap. The letters are equally distributed among the caps.
If you collect all five letters, you get a bottle of juice at half price.
Estimate how many bottles you need to buy to collect all five letters.

Read   What do you want to find? *You want to find how many bottles
            of juice you need to buy to collect all five letters.*

Plan   Instead of actually buying bottles of juice,
            develop a simulation. You can use a five-part
            spinner. Spin until you get all five letters. Keep
            track of your results.

Solve   Show the results of the simulation in a list. You
            spun the spinner 7 times before you got all five
            letters. So you estimate that you would have to
            buy 7 bottles of juice to collect all five letters.

Spins
I J I C U J E

Look Back   Would you get the same result if you repeat the simulation?

Solve by simulating the problem. Describe your simulation.

1. There is one of ten team cards inside
   a box of cereal. The teams are equally
   distributed among the boxes.
   Estimate how many boxes of cereal
   you need to purchase to collect all ten
   teams.

   _____

   _____

   _____

2. There is one of five shapes on the
   inner wrapper of each granola bar.
   The symbols are equally distributed
   among the wrappers. Estimate how
   many bars you need to buy to collect
   all five shapes and win a free bar.

   _____

   _____

   _____

3. A gas station gives away one of eight
   drinking glasses each time you buy a
   tank of gas. There is an equal chance
   of getting any one of the glasses.
   Estimate how many tanks you will
   have to buy to get all eight glasses.

   _____

   _____

   _____

4. A store prints one of 12 different
   symbols on each receipt. Collect all 12
   and you get a 10% discount on your
   next purchase. Symbols are equally
   placed among the receipts. Estimate
   how many receipts you would have
   to get to collect all 12 symbols.

   _____

   _____

   _____

Reteaching 2: Simulations

When you use simulation to solve a problem, you must first develop a model. Then, conduct experiments to generate data.

You and a friend are equally skilled at playing checkers. Estimate how many games you will have to play until one of you wins 6 games.

Read   What do you want to find? *You want to find out how many games of checkers you can expect to play until one of you wins six games.*

Plan   Instead of actually playing the games, develop a simulation. You can toss a coin to see who wins each game. Heads means you win. Tails means your friend wins. Keep track of your results.

Solve   Show the results of the simulation in a table. You tossed the coin 10 times before either 6 heads or 6 tails appeared. So you estimate that you would have to play 10 games before one of you would win 6 games.

Tosses of a Coin	
Result	**Number**
Heads	$\cancel{||||}$ $|$
Tails	$||||$

Look Back Do you think you would get the same results if you repeated the simulation?

Describe a simulation you could use to solve each problem.

1. There is one of four symbols on the inner wrapper of energy bars. The symbols are equally distributed among the wrappers. If you collect all four symbols, you get a free bar. Estimate how many bars you need to purchase to win a free bar.

   _____
   _____
   _____

2. A bakery puts a saying in each cookie. There are 36 different sayings, and there is an equally likely chance that any one of them will be inside any cookie. Estimate how many cookies Mary would have to buy to collect all 36 sayings.

   _____
   _____
   _____

3. A bank gives away one of six baseball cards each time you make a deposit. There is an equal chance of getting any one of the cards. Estimate how many deposits you will have to make to get all six cards.

   _____
   _____

4. Your 10 pairs of socks are in the dryer. Each pair of socks is a different color. Estimate how many socks you will have to pull out without looking to get two the same color.

   _____
   _____

Name _____ Class _____ Date _____

Practice 1: Simulations

Solve by simulating the problem. Show your work.

You and your partner play a game in which you each toss a coin. You score a point for each head and your partner scores a point for each tail. The first person to score ten points wins.

1. **a.** The score is 7 to 9 in favor of your partner when you must stop. If you continue the game later, what is the probability that you will win? (*Hint:* Think of how many turns the game may last.) _____

   b. What is the probability that your partner will win? _____

2. **a.** The score is 7 to 8 in your favor when you must stop. If you continue the game later, what is the probability that you will win? (*Hint:* Think of how many turns the game may last.) _____

   b. What is the probability that your partner will win? _____

A weather forecaster reports that the probability for sunny weather each day for the next few days is 50%. You begin a three-day camping trip.

3. Simulate the situation to find the probability of three sunny days in a row.

   _____

4. Simulate the situation to find the probability of only two sunny days out of the three.

   _____

5. Simulate the situation to find the probability of only one sunny day out of the three.

   _____

6. Simulate the situation to find the probability of no sun for any of the three days.

   _____

A basketball player scores a basket on about 1 out of every 6 shots.

7. Explain how you could use a number cube to simulate the player's shooting average.

   _____

8. Use your simulation to find the probability of the player making 4 out of 5 of her next shots. _____

Practice 2: Simulations

Describe a simulation you could use to solve each problem.

1. A grocery store is running a contest. Every time you enter the store, you receive a card with the letter W, I, N, E, or R. You have an equally likely chance of receiving any one card. To win a prize, you must spell WINNER by collecting the cards. How many times will you have to enter the store to win a prize?

_____

_____

2. A sugarless-gum company wraps its product in a piece of paper with one of the digits 1 to 6 on the paper. When you collect wrappers that contain all 6 digits, you win a prize. Use a number cube to help you decide how many pieces of gum you will need to buy in order to get all 6 digits.

_____

_____

Use any strategy to solve each problem. Show your work.

3. In 1960, the submarine *Triton* traveled 36,014 miles journeying around the world. If the trip took 76 days, how many miles did the *Triton* average each day?

_____

4. After working for a company for a year, Melanie received a 10% raise in her salary. Later, the entire company took a 10% cut in pay because of budget difficulties. If Melanie started working at $2,000 a month, what would she now be receiving?

_____

5. At the mall on Saturday, Suki bought a pair of blue jeans for $15.55 and some books for $8.53. For lunch she spent $1.50 on juice and $3.25 on a sandwich. When she left the mall she had $5.27 left. How much money did Suki take to the mall?

_____

6. Mari plans to make a doll's quilt with 16 squares. Half of the squares will be solid red. The rest of the squares will be half calico print and half white. If each square is 9 inches on a side, how many square feet of each type of fabric will she need?

_____

Assessment 7: Statistical Investigations and Simulations

•••

1. Which would be the best sample of the population for an automobile manufacturer to survey to learn what car buyers in your town think of its newest cars? Explain your answer.

   A. Every 20th person to enter a certain fast-food restaurant in town.
   B. The first 100 people waiting in line to buy tickets to a concert.
   C. Registered drivers in town selected randomly by computer.
   D. Everyone who visits the car showroom on Saturday morning.

   _____

   _____

2. Is the question "What do you think of the President's new economic program?" open or closed? Fair or unfair? Explain.

   _____

   _____

3. In a survey at the mall, 65 people, representing 25% of the sample, responded that they prefer watching movies at a theater rather than on television. How many people were surveyed? _____

4. People entering the baseball park were asked if they would give one dollar to a local charity. Of the first 24 patrons, 16 agreed to give the dollar. If 30,000 people attend the baseball game, estimate how much money will be raised based on the sample. _____

5. The 750 students at the dance will each have a choice of one iced tea or one lemonade. The beverage committee polled 20 students and found that the probability that a person would pick a given drink was $\frac{1}{2}$. The committee is concerned that if there are 375 of each drink, they may run out of one of the drinks. They are willing to buy some extra drinks, but they don't want to buy more extras than they need. They do a simulation, flipping a coin 75 times:

   H L H H L H L H L L H H L L H H L H L H L L L H L H H
   H L L L L H H L H H H H L H H H H L L H L H L H H H L L H
   H H L L H H L H L H L H L L L H L L H H L H H H H L H

   Explain how the coin flips can simulate the drink problem. Based on the simulation, how many extra drinks of each type should they buy for each student to have his or her first-choice beverage?

   _____

   _____

Cumulative Assessment

• •

1. Chris is figuring out how to budget the money she earns babysitting. She expects to make about $15 a week, and lists her major expenses below.

   Transportation $4
   Food $5
   Books and CDs $5

   Everything else is too small to list individually. Draw an appropriate graph showing Chris's budget.

2. Zak's math test scores are: 86, 88, 79, 88 and 93. Find the mean, median, and mode.

   _____

3. A marathoner's race times (in hours and minutes) were: 3:44, 3:57, 3:42, 5:01, 3:51. Explain which measure of central tendency gives the best sense of the runner's performance.

   _____

   _____

4. The median of five numbers is 27. Four of the numbers are 10, 24, 27, and 30. What is the fifth number? _____

5. The mean of five numbers is 27. Four of the numbers are 10, 24, 27, and 30. What is the fifth number? _____

6. Explain how a graph can present data in a misleading way.

   _____

   _____

   _____

7. Evaluate $_7C_3$ and $_7P_3$.

   _____

8. How many different ways can the letters MATHTEST be arranged?

   _____

9. A combination lock has the numbers 0 to 9 on each dial. The lock comes with 3 or 4 dials. How many more combinations are possible with the 4-dial lock?

   _____

Cumulative Assessment (cont.)

10. A multiple-choice test has four possible answers to each question. What are the chances of getting the first four questions right just by guessing ?

_____

11. A family has four children. What are the chances that the children's gender alternates so that there are no two boys or two girls in a row?

_____

12. What are the chances of drawing a pair from a shuffled deck of cards?

_____

13. What are the chances of drawing a pair of aces from a shuffled deck of cards?

_____

14. What are the chances of drawing two aces if you replace the first card?

_____

15. Sundaes can be made with chocolate or vanilla ice cream, hot fudge or butterscotch sauce, and whipped cream or marshmallow topping. How many different kinds of sundaes are there?

_____

16. A policeman observes 2 out of 10 cars fail to come to a full stop at a stop sign. How many stop sign violations should he predict in a day if 800 cars pass the sign?

_____

17. Carl rolls a number cube 300 times and gets a 6 48 times. What are the experimental and theoretical probabilities for rolling a six?

_____

18. Give an example of a biased question that could be used to survey students' favorite pizza. Re-write the question to be fair.

_____

19. A random sample of 36 people in town found that 12 of them like chocolate milk. If there are 120,000 people in town, how many would be expected to like chocolate milk based on the sampling?

_____